THE
LIFE AND TIMES
OF THE
NAWABS
OF LUCKNOW

❧ THE ❧
LIFE AND TIMES
OF THE
NAWABS
OF LUCKNOW

Ravi Bhatt *R.R.Bhatt*

Rupa & Co

Dedication
For the people promoting peace between India and Pakistan

Text © Ravi Bhatt 2006

Design Copyright © Rupa & Co. 2006

Published in 2006 by

Rupa . Co

7/16, Ansari Road, Daryaganj
New Delhi 110 002

Sales Centres :
Allahabad Bangalore Chandigarh Chennai
Hyderabad Jaipur Kathmandu
Kolkata Mumbai Pune

Cover & Book Design by
Kapil Gupta
kapilkgupta@hotmail.com

Printed in India by
Gopsons Paper Ltd.
A-14, Sector-60
Noida 201 301

Contents

Preface

The greatest civilisations of the world have been shaped by the regional cultures they encompassed, and the Indian civilisation was no exception. Universally acknowledged as the hub of rich cultural manifestation, it too is indebted to its many regions in the subcontinent.

Lucknow is just a dot on the world map, but its sophisticated and refined culture, evolved over the years, has contributed considerably to the composite Indian culture. In fact, though this culture originated with the Mughal dynasty, which ruled from Delhi, it was promoted, patronised and taken to its zenith by the rulers of Awadh, better known as the Nawabs of Lucknow. These Nawabs were initially administrative cogs in the Mughul Empire, but in the year 1819, the seventh Nawab, Ghazi-ud-din Haidar, snapped ties with Delhi and declared himself an independent king. In practice though, even after their rebellion, they continued to be referred to as Nawabs, rather than kings.

It is interesting to note that the rulers of Lucknow, probably one of their kind, are remembered not so much for their war victories, but for the unique culture they espoused. This culture, without a trace of imperiousness, advanced a secular tradition that nurtured communal harmony and respect for others' feelings and faith. It was due to the strong influence of this culture that Lucknow never witnessed any communal riots, not even during Partition. This clearly proves that Lucknow's culture succeeded where the best of sermons failed.

The book tries to bring alive the colourful and idiosyncratic lifestyle of the Nawabs of Lucknow, who, knowingly and unknowingly, wove the fabric of this peerless culture.

VIEW OF LUCKNOW

An Overview

Lucknow is located in a region called Awadh, which was one of the twelve subas, or provinces, of the Mughal emperor Akbar. The word 'Awadh' is derived from 'Ayodhya', the Hindu holy city, situated on the banks of River Ghagra (also known as Saryu), which flows through the region. 'Ayodhya' in Sanskrit means 'unconquerable'. According to the epic the *Ramayana*, Ayodhya was Lord Rama's capital. References suggest that Lord Rama, at the time of his coronation after returning from fourteen years of exile, had given his younger brother Lakshman the reins of the region, being referred to here as Lucknow.

The editor of *Gazetteer of Lucknow*, H.R. Neville, records that, as per legend, Tharus and low-caste Hindus like Kurmis, Muraos, Passis, Arakhs and Bhars initially ruled the region of Awadh. Their principality remained under the great Bhar Dynasty of Behraich till 1093 AD. Between the eleventh and the fifteenth century, Rajput clans, such as Solankis, Panwars, Chauhans and Bais, started dominating the scene. Muslims too began their inroads into the region, with the invasion led by Bakhtiyar Khilji.

For about eighty-four years (from 1394 to 1478) Awadh was part of the Sharaqi kingdom of Jaunpur in present-day Uttar Pradesh; Emperor Humayun made it a part of the Mughal Empire around 1555. During Emperor Jehangir's rule, he granted an estate in Awadh to a nobleman, Sheik Abdul Rahim, who had won his favour. Sheik Abdul Rahim later built Machchi Bhawan in this estate; this later became the seat of power from where his descendants, the Sheikhzades, controlled the region.

Nawab — the plural of the Arabic word 'naib', meaning 'assistant' — was the term given to governors appointed by the Mughal emperor all over India to assist him in managing the Empire.

In the absence of expeditious transport and communication facilities, they were practically independent rulers of their territory and wielded the power of life and death over their subjects. The Nawabs of Lucknow were in fact the Nawabs of Awadh, but were so referred to because, after the reign of the third Nawab, Lucknow became the capital of their realm.

The Nawabi period, for which Lucknow is famous far and wide, started on 9 September 1722 when the Mughal Emperor Mohammad Shah shifted Saadat Khan from Agra, where he had failed to control the Jats, and appointed him as subedar of Awadh. This transfer proved lucky for Saadat Khan, as he not only successfully consolidated his position in Lucknow against the stiff resistance offered by the Sheikhzades, but also founded the legendary Awadh dynasty, which lasted till 1856.

After establishing himself in Awadh, Saadat Khan began fighting wars for the emperor again. He committed suicide after losing a battle against the invader Nadir Shah. After Saadat Khan's death, his son-in-law, Safdar Jung, took his place on the recommendation of Nadir Shah. Safdar Jung, who had established Faizabad, was very close to the emperor, and held important positions in the Delhi court. On Safdar Jung's death in 1754, his son Shuja-ud-daulah became Nawab. One of the most crucial incidents of his rule was his defeat in the battle of Buxar against the British, in which he was forced to compromise on very humiliating terms. However, Shuja-ud-daulah is better known for initiating the cultural practices for which Lucknow eventually became renowned. He started the practice of inviting and patronising artists, poets, courtesans and writers from different parts of the country, primarily Delhi.

Next in the lineage of dynastic rule was his son Nawab Asif-ud-daulah, who had shifted his capital from Faizabad to Lucknow. He will always be remembered in history for two reasons: first, his construction of what is arguably the most famous and magnificent building in Lucknow, the Bara Imambara, and second, his exploitation of family members for money. His son, Nawab Wazir Ali's rule was also marked by two features: egregious expenditure for his marriage ceremony, and his extremely short rule comprising just four months from 21 September 1797 to 21 January 1798. His rule was truncated by the British who removed him in their own interests. He was succeeded by Asif-ud-daulah's brother Nawab Saadat Ali Khan, a man who had had absolutely no chance of ascending the throne. Political compulsions, however, had worked in his favour. Historical reports say that, at one time, a disillusioned Saadat Ali Khan wanted to abdicate. His magnificent mausoleum lies in the heart of Lucknow.

The seventh Nawab, Ghazi-ud-din Haidar, was also the first king of Awadh as he severed all ties with the emperor and declared himself sovereign. The British considered his successor, Nawab Nasir-ud-din Haidar, a ridiculous ruler. Haidar had taken up the most ambitious engineering project of that period, that of connecting two rivers, which unfortunately failed because of faulty planning.

After Nasir-ud-din Haidar, Mohammad Ali Shah was installed on the throne by the British at the ripe old age of about sixty. Like Saadat Ali Khan, it was luck that got him the throne. His son Amjad Ali Shah, the tenth Nawab, was the most religious Nawab and for this reason was called Hazrat. He tried to run the administration on religious lines.

The last ruler of the dynasty was Nawab Wajid Ali Shah. He was the most colourful and culturally evolved ruler of all. He had penned more than a hundred books in Urdu and Persian. Unfortunately, the British — wanting to expand their empire — first defamed the Nawab as a debauch and inefficient ruler and then, on the instructions of Governor-General Dalhousie, British Resident J. Outram on 4 February met Wajid Ali and asked him to sign an agreement. According to this agreement, he had to surrender his kingdom to the British in exchange of an annual pension of Rs 12 lakh, and an additional Rs 3 lakh per year for the servants. He was also entitled to retain the title of king. Wajid Ali refused to sign this agreement. Outram, as per instructions, gave him three days to give in. After three days, on 7 February 1856, Outram dethroned him and his kingdom was annexed on the pretext of misrule.

Thus ended the great Nawab dynasty, which produced a culture that still lingers in the every day life of Lucknow.

Palace Politics

The First Nawab's Last Decision

The first ruler of Awadh and the founder of the Awadh dynasty, Meer Mohammad Ameen, later referred to in history as Saadat Khan, was appointed as the subedar of Awadh by the Delhi court on 9 September 1722. He was once a resident of Nishapur, Iran, and like many of his countrymen, specially the nobility, he felt frustrated and alienated by the rampant corruption of the ruling class. He came to India around the year 1708–9, to seek his fortune.

Meer Mohammad Ameen's father, Meer Mohammad Naseer, and elder brother, Meer Mohammad Dagar, had already come to India and settled in Patna. Unfortunately, when Meer Mohammad reached Patna, he discovered that his father had long passed away.

He travelled on to Delhi, and with the help of Rai Ratan Chand, the Diwan of Qutbul Mulk Nawab Abdullah Khan, he gained access to Emperor Farukh Siyar's court. At this juncture, he conspired against Qutbul Mulk and played a crucial role in the assassination of his brother, Syed Hasan Ali. In his book, *Nightfall of Mughal Empire*, S.K. Sharma writes that Mughal Emperor Mohammad Shah rewarded Meer Mohammad with the governorship of Agra and the title of 'Saadat Khan Burhan-ul-Mulk'. In 1722, when Saadat Khan, as he was now called, failed to subdue the Jats of the region, he was transferred to Awadh as subedar.

At this time, the Sunni Sheikhzades of Lucknow were very powerful and were rebelling against Delhi. It is said that the Sheikhzades had hung a sword at the Sheikhan gate of their palace and issued orders that anyone who entered the building must salute the sword.

The Sheikhzades decided to oppose Saadat Khan, and there are two different versions of how the new Nawab defeated them. According to the first account, Saadat Khan managed to get the

The founder of the Awadh dynasty, Saadat Khan

help of the Sunni Sheikhs of Kakori and, instead of coming to Lucknow through Mahmood Nagar and Akbari Gate where the Sheikhzades were waiting to fight him, he changed route and arrived in Lucknow by crossing the river Gomati at Gaughat. He managed to capture Machchi Bhawan, the stronghold of the Sheikhzades, without any resistance. Riding on an elephant, he cut the cord with which the sword was hung at the gate as a symbol of the Sheikhzades' authority.

According to the second account, Saadat Khan camped at Mahmood Nagar and invited the Sheikhzades for a feast. While the enemy was enjoying his hospitality, Saadat Khan's army captured Lucknow and Machchi Bhawan.

After consolidating his power in Awadh, Saadat Khan married off his daughter to his nephew, Safdar Jung, who was also appointed his deputy, leaving the Nawab free to again become active in the power games in Delhi.

Saadat Khan fought and won many battles for the Mughal Emperor. In 1738, when Nadir Shah of Persia was at the borders of Lahore, as per standard practice, Saadat Khan was called to resist the impending invasion. Although Saadat Khan's army was tired at the time, having been on the move for the last one month, he went ahead to check Nadir Shah's advance. He fought with courage, but lost the battle. He was almost killed, but a soldier in Nadir Shah's army who happened to be from Saadat Khan's native place in Iran, went near his elephant and saved him. A wounded and captive Saadat Khan was produced before Nadir Shah.

When Nadir Shah asked him why he had chosen to attack him first, although he was a Saiyyad and from the same faith and same native country, Saadat Khan replied intelligently. He said, had he not done so, 'all the chiefs and nobles of Hindustan would have accused me that I was in treacherous league with Your Majesty, and the very term "Persian" would have been an object of scorn in this country.'

Nadir Shah, impressed by his reply, softened towards Saadat Khan. He was about to retreat with a 'gift' of Rs 50 lakh, but unfortunately for Saadat Khan and Delhi, things took an unexpected turn.

Saadat Khan got the news that Samsam-ud-daulah Khan Dauran, who held the post of Mir Bakhshi, had suddenly died and the post had been given to his colleague, Nizam-ul-Mulk Qulich Khan, with the indirect consent of the emperor. This news upset Saadat Khan as the post had been promised to him. Out of jealousy, he instigated Nadir Shah to march upon Delhi. Saadat Khan told Nadir Shah that the amount of Rs 50 lakhs, which he had received from him in the way of compensation from the emperor, was a small sum from the Mughal emperor, considering that Saadat Khan himself could have paid a similar amount from his own territory, Awadh.

He tempted Nadir Shah with a promise to extort about Rs 20 crores from Delhi. Nadir Shah decided to take a chance. He appointed Saadat Khan as the vakil-i-mutlaq and asked him to take the charge of Delhi. Later on, Delhi was completely destroyed by Nadir Shah. Nadir Shah had gone with his army to Delhi to collect money. In Delhi, a rumour suddenly spread that Nadir Shah had died, so a mob attacked one of his troops of 3,000 people. A bullet narrowly missed Nadir Shah himself when he was going to the mosque to pray. Nadir Shah retaliated by ordering a general massacre in which several thousands of innocent people were killed and large-scale properties were destroyed. Nadir Shah also sent his men to Awadh to bring Sadat Khan's money. Humiliated by Nadir Shah, Saadat Khan committed suicide on 20 March 1739.

Saadat Khan's Successor

After Nawab Saadat Khan committed suicide, a fight for the throne quickly ensued, as he did not have a son. One claimant was his brother's son, Muazam Sher Jung. The other was his sister's son, Mirza Mohammad Muqeem Khan, who later took the name of Safdar Jung. Mohammad Muqeem Khan was married to Saadat Khan's daughter, Sadrunnisa.

The dispute was resolved after Mohammad Muqeem Khan bribed Nadir Shah with Rs 20 million: the Afghan instructed Emperor Mohammad Shah in Delhi to appoint Mohammad Muqeem Khan as the subedar of Awadh.

Mohammad Muqeem Khan, who adopted the name Safdar Jung at this point, returned to his capital Ayodhya a happy man. He believed that his ascension was a divine gift and so renamed his residence from 'Bungla' (bungalow) to 'Faizabad', coined by joining two words 'Faiza', meaning profit, and 'Abad', meaning population. Faizabad soon developed into an impressive city, and is still known by this name today. There was another reason why Safdar Jung named the city Faizabad: the name of the small town in the Khurasan province of Iran that he was from, was also called Faizabad; it was a town that enjoyed very good climate and was famous for its watermelons.

Possibly, Saadat Khan had wanted his son-in-law to succeed him. In what seemed to be an effort to groom him on these lines, he had first posted him in the army, and later on made him naib (assistant) subedar. In 1739, when Saadat Khan went to Delhi to fight against Nadir Shah, he gave the charge of Awadh to Safdar Jung.

Nawab Safdar Jung was an ambitious ruler and played his cards very well in the game of power. At the Mughal court, he

Nawab Safdar Jung

played so important a role that he was soon made the Mir Atish (chief of artillery) of the Empire. He also made efforts to expand his territory: when Nawab Imdulmulk was murdered by his own servant, Safdar Jung promptly annexed the victim's territory, Allahabad, to Awadh.

Interestingly, Nawab Safdar Jung was at one time appointed the subedar of Kashmir as well. This meant he was expected to simultaneously govern areas that were hundreds of miles apart. Later, Safdar Jung got the subadari of Kashmir transferred to his competitor and cousin, Sher Jung.

How strong and unchallenged a position Safdar Jung briefly enjoyed, can be judged by the following incident. In 1748, when Emperor Mohammad Shah was on the Mughal throne, the Afghans attacked India. The emperor sent his son Ahmad Shah, along with Wazir Qamruddin Khan, Raja Jai Singh Sawai and Safdar Jung, to lead the battle against them. Safdar Jung performed exceptionally well and Abdali and his Afghani forces were successfully repelled. At this juncture, Prince Ahmad Shah promised Safdar Jung, that, when he became king, he would, as reward, make Safdar Jung his prime minister.

However, when Ahmad Shah succeeded his father after the latter's demise on 15 April 1748, he forgot his promise; he considered appointing the Nizam of Hyderabad as his prime minister. This was very disappointing for Safdar Jung, but, instead of losing heart, he formed a faction that put intense pressure on the king. At last, on 29 June 1748, he was appointed Wazir, prime minister, by Ahmed Shah.

Unfortunately, this legendary Nawab became the victim of court intrigues spearheaded by Iranian and Turanis groups at the emperor's court; he returned to Awadh in 1753, where he died the next year on 5 October 1754 in district Sultanpur on the banks of River Gomati at Paparghat. His body was brought to Gulab Bari at Faizabad, where it was interred. Later, the remains of Safdar Jung were shifted to Delhi where his son, Shuja-ud-daulah, constructed an imposing tomb at the cost of three lakh rupees. The entire area around this tomb in New Delhi is still officially known as Safdarjung.

King for Three-and-a-half Hours

After the death of the eighth Nawab, Nasir-ud-din Haider, on 8 July 1837 (he was allegedly poisoned by a favourite, trusted maidservant, Dhania Kahari), there was chaos in the kingdom. The British wanted to install the late king's sixty-year-old crippled and rheumatic uncle, Mohammed Ali on the throne, while Nasir-ud-din Haider's mother wanted her grandson, seventeen-year-old son Munna Jan (whose paternity was controversial), on the throne.

The British set a date for the coronation of Mohammad Ali. On the day, the old man lay resting in the Farhat Bakhsh palace with his relatives, including his grandson, Wajid Ali Shah, when Badsha Begum approached the palace with 2,000 of her supporters. Standing at the gate — which had been closed by the British —Captain Paton tried to reason with the begum. Before he could get a reply from her however, her armed supporters brought an elephant to force down the gate. The first attempt failed, but in the second attempt, the elephant broke the gate. The furious and confused crowd rushed inside the palace, beat Captain Paton with the hilts of their swords and butts of their guns, and installed Munna Jan on the throne while Badsha Begum sat at its foot in an enclosed palanquin.

John Pemble in his book, *The Raj, the Indian Mutiny, and the Kingdom Of Oudh,* observes, that 'the next three and a half hours were critical'. The situation was undoubtedly out of the ordinary. According to Ursula Low in *Fifty Years with Johan Company*: 'The dead king lay in one chamber; Mohammad Ali waiting for his coronation, sat cowering for his life in another; while a furious mob of mat-locked men and dancing girls filled the great hall with loud and mad acclamation in honour of Munna Jan and Badsha Begum.'

During all this confusion, some of the begum's followers got hold of the British Resident by his collar, dragged him to the throne, and, on threat of instant death, ordered him to congratulate Munna Jan. Badsha Begum's advocate somehow rescued the Captain.

At last, Brigadier Johanstone arrived with his force, and the Resident, holding his watch in his hand, gave the begum warning to vacate the hall within fifteen minutes. After the said time was up, his forces opened fire in which, as per British accounts, thirty to forty people, and as per native estimates, five hundred people, died. The newly-appointed king, Munna Jan, was arrested from a small recess under the throne. He and Badsha Begum were eventually sent to Chunar Fort as prisoners and Mohammad Ali was installed as king of Awadh.

The Culture of Coins

Through the ages, the issuance of coins has been associated with a ruler's authority. Apart from the needs of the economy, it was also motivated by the ruler's desire to keep his name and legacy alive for posterity. This was the reason why, when a water-carrier was made king for a day by a grateful emperor in Delhi, he exercised his prerogative and issued leather currency (in those days water-carriers used leather bags to carry water).

Historian G.D. Bhatnagar mentions in his work *Awadh under Wajid Ali Shah*, that the Nawab's royal mint was located at Akhtarnagar. While, this might give the impression that the mint was at a locality named Akhtarnagar, in fact, according to Mirza Ali Azhar, it is a reference to Lucknow. The city was popularly known as Akhtarnagar after Wajid Ali Shah's pseudonym (takhallus) 'Akhtar', but it could not replace the old name of the city. Therefore both the names, Akhtarnagar and Lucknow, are mentioned on his coins. The mint was located to the west of present-day Nakhkhas, which is even today called Mohalla Taksal in Lucknow.

Maharaja Jai Gopal 'Saqib' writes in his book *Zubdat-ul-Kawaef* that this mint was supervised by Rajadhiraj Pradhan Raja Rao Umrao Singh.

Durign Wajid Ali Shah's nine-year rule, it was the practice to issue currency in the month of Muharram. Coins were denominated as muhars, half-muhars, silver rupees, two-annas, annas, pice, half-pice and quarter-pice. On the reverse side of the coins was written 'Mulk-e-Awadh bait-us-saltant Akhtar-nagar Lucknow', meaning House of the Government of Awadh, Akhtarnagar, Lucknow. The different kinds of rupees in circulation were Farrukhabadi rupee, Wajid Ali Shah's rupee, Bang-e-Shahi rupee, Machhli Shahi rupee, Shamsher Shahi rupee, Putli Shahi rupee, Puri Shahi rupee.

It was the practice for coins of previous years and reigns to be accepted at a discounted rate. For example, King Ghazi-ud-din Haidar's rupee was discounted at the rate of seven damris, while Nawab Saadat Ali Khan's period rupee, six 'dams'.

The Fall of Nawab Wazir Ali

The change that time can bring to the fortunes of a man has no better illustration than the life of the fifth Nawab, Wazir Ali.

His father, Nawab Asif-ud-daulah, had declared him his successor in the presence of the Governor-General, Lord Hastings, and the British Resident. Wazir Ali's marriage was one of the most opulent shows of wealth and power in the annals of Awadh. This grand show was organised with the active help of important persons like Raja Tikait Rai, Almas Khan, Jawahar Ali Khan, Tahseen Ali Khan, Allama Tafazzul Husain Khan and Bahu Begum. In a rare gesture, very uncharacteristic of the Nawabs, Nawab Asif-ud-daulah walked for a short distance in front of his son's marriage procession. When the courtier insisted he ride on something, he said: 'Today I wish to walk like my subordinates in front of Wazir Ali.' This wedding was the most expensive one in the history of the Nawabs and at par with wedding ceremonies of the royals of Delhi. It cost Rs 36 lakhs, and this in the eighteenth century.

Wazir Ali ascended the throne on 21 September 1797, after the death of his father. But it was just four months before he ran out of luck. He failed to keep the people around him happy and the same people — Tikait Rai, Allama Tafuzzal Husain Khan, Tahseen Ali Khan, Almas Khan and his grandmother Bahu Begum — who had helped organise his marriage, successfully planned his downfall. Just four months after being crowned, on 21 January 1798, he was not only dethroned but arrested by the British and sent to Banaras (Varanasi). The Governor-General orchestrated this while holding a darbar at Bibapur Palace. One of the reasons for the arrest was that the British suspected that Wazir Ali had anti-British leanings. Also, there were rumours about his paternity, although historians like H.C. Irwin believe that Wazir Ali was probably Asif-ud-daulah's legitimate son.

The fifth Nawab, Wazir Ali

While in Banaras, Wazir Ali felt that the East India Company's Resident in that city was contributing to his misfortune. So, in a fit of rage, he killed the Resident G. F. Cherry. While reports are conflicting regarding where he was imprisoned —Chunar Garh or Fort William at Calcutta — it is certain that Wazir Ali died while in jail in 1817. And, while his wedding cost Rs 36 lakhs, his funeral expenses were met with just seventy rupees.

A Pawn becomes King

Once, the Emperor of India did not permit the British Governor-General of India Marquis of Hastings to sit in his presence, despite a request by the latter. The piqued Governor-General decided to avenge his humiliation by chalking out a strategy that would belittle the emperor. He instigated the seventh Nawab of Awadh, Ghazi-ud-din Haidar, to declare himself king in defiance of Delhi. Sir Henry Lawrence, a British who had come to Lucknow in 1857 and played a decisive role in the first war of independence, recorded that Lord Hastings had calculated that, by encouraging Nawab Ghaz-iud-din Haidar to use the title of king, he could create a rivalry between the rulers of Awadh and Delhi. James Mill has also written in *A History of British India* that Ghazi-ud-din, with the consent of the Governor-General, assumed the title and style of king. Hastings was wily though: while he gave Haidar the status of royalty to settle a personal score with Delhi, he also took some monetary consideration from the Nawab in return for the new standing.

This is not the end of the story. Two of the emperor's brothers lived in Lucknow. Before the Nawabs were given new status, it was tradition that, if they came across the Nawab while on the road, the elephant on which Nawab was riding would have to kneel down to show respect. The British suggested to the Nawab that he cease such practices as they were degrading to his newly acquired status, equal to the emperor.

According to M. Najmul Ghani Rampuri in *Tareekh-e-Awadh* and S. Kamaluddeen Haidar in *Quaisar-ut-Tawareekh*, Ghazi-ud-din was sent a crest with two lions carrying an insignia, as mark of extreme regard, by the Marquis of Hastings. Ghazi-ud-din obligingly accepted it and the original family insignia of the Awadh dynasty — the fish — was placed between the two lions.

Nawab Ghazi-ud-din Haidar

Traditional royal emblem of Awadh adopted during the time of Saadat Khan

Ghazi-ud-din asked for permission to use this new insignia on the coins of Awadh. He was told that he had full powers within his kingdom and the British would not interfere.

On 19 October 1819, Ghazi-ud-din formally discontinued his subordination to the Mughal emperor and declared himself independent king. The British, to insult the emperor, goaded the Nawab to send newly issued coins along with his proclamation of independence to Delhi. The Mughals perceived this as treachery. They replied with a Persian couplet:

Ghazi-ud-din's changed royal emblem after declaring himself independent king

Thanks to heaven's atrocity coins have been issued

by Ghazi-ud-din Haidar the treacherous King

Why the Prime Minister was not Punished

Nawabi culture, for which Lucknow was known all over the civilised world, was the creation of a unique set of social and political forces. It is natural that such a colourful period should witness many interesting events.

The seventh Nawab, and the first king of Awadh, Ghazi-ud-din Haidar, thought that experience in a royal household was a suitable qualification for a prime minister. After becoming the ruler of Awadh in 1814, Ghazi-ud-din appointed Agha Mir — one of his favourites who had earlier served as khansama (supervisor / steward / cook) of Nawab Saadat Ali Khan — as his prime minister.

Writer Bishop Reginald Herber describes Agha Mir as 'a dark, harsh, hawk-nosed man, with an expression of mouth which seems to imply habitual self-command struggling with a naturally rough temper.'

Except for a brief period, Agha Mir — who was given the title 'Moatam-ud-daula' meaning 'Pillar of the State' by Ghazi-ud-din — served the king till his death in 1827. The short period of disfavour that Agha suffered, was due to the devious planning of his political rival, Hakim Mehdi Ali Khan.

The king was so fond of Agha Mir, that he deposited a crore of rupees at the rate of five percent with the East India Company, on the condition that a particular portion of the interest would be regularly paid to Agha Mir, his wife, son, daughter and family as pension. The total amount as pension to Agha Mir's family added up to Rs 25,000 a year. There was one more condition attached: the Company would protect the life, honour and property of Agha and his family, as personages 'guaranteed' against the future rulers of Awadh.

Prime Minister Agha Mir

Agha Mir was astute and knew how to win the confidence of his master. He successfully created a rift between Badsha Begum and the king to his advantage. Ghazi-ud-din was an easy-going person with a fondness for sensual pleasures. Agha Mir cleverly exploited this weakness of the Nawab, to fill his own coffers with money from the state exchequer. He, along with other courtiers and the British officials at the Residency, also cornered a cut on all commercial deals of the state.

It is said that, while selecting precious stones for the king's crown at the time of his coronation, about one-fourth of the royal collection was pilfered. Agha was so shrewd that, as he unscrupulously went about amassing unheard of wealth, he was, at the same time, able to gain the king's confidence completely.

When his involvement in financial irregularities came to light, the king was on his deathbed. So fond of Agha Mir was he, Ghazi-ud-din absolved Agha of all responsibility for the embezzlement.

Aware of Agha Mir's misdeeds, the next ruler, Nasir-ud-din Haidar, dismissed him on 20 December 1828. He wanted to punish and recover money from Agha Mir, but failed because the British protected him on the pretext that he and his family were under immunity granted to 'guaranteed person[s]' of the Company.

Finally, the cook turned prime minister, Agha Mir, with his ill-gotten wealth of about twenty-five million sterling loaded in about eight hundred carts, was safely escorted by the Company troops out of the kingdom, and the king could do nothing.

The Minister-Maker

'Her ... anger was so violent that her husband had to submit to her will for fear...' writes the biographer Abdul Ahad. W.H. Sleeman, in his work *A Journey through the Kingdom of Oudh*, comments: 'Her own frequent ebullitions, which often disfigured the King's robes and vests, and left even the hair on his head and chin unsafe...'

These uncharitable remarks were made about the first queen of Awadh, Badsha Begum, who was one of the most learned begums of the Awadh dynasty. Born in 1777 in a reputed Rizvi Saiyyad family, she was provided excellent opportunities by her father, Mubashshir Khan Munajjam-ul-mulk, to learn literature, astronomy and theology.

Her beauty and education impressed the sixth ruler of Awadh, Saadat Ali Khan, and when once she visited Varanasi along with her father, he proposed a Dola marriage between his son, Ghazi-ud-din Haidar, and Badsha Begum. Her father turned down this offer, as the Dola form of marriage — performed without a marriage procession and considered lower in status than a Nikah — was not acceptable to him. Saadat Ali finally agreed to a Nikah because his scholar son, Ghazi-ud-din, liked Badsha Begum and Saadat Ali thought it wise not to miss the opportunity.

While quite a few historians write censoriously about her, Captain White writes about her in *The Murdered King of Oudh* as 'one of the most wonderful women of the world'. There are many scholars who thought she was ahead of her times. Abdul Ahad, author of *Tarikh-I-Badsha Begum,* describes her as '[not of a] slavish mentality to overrate [a] man, [however] greatly superior in calibre or physique, to submit to [his] whims and wishes.'

This self-respecting begum did not spare anyone, including ministers, who tried to act against her wishes. The first minister of Awadh who was sacked on her advice, was Agha Mir, whose mistake had been to hog the limelight in a meeting with the Governor-General, Lord Moira, overshadowing the heir apparent, Sulaiman Jah. Her second victim was minister Mirza Haji, who had succeeded Agha Mir. He had helped her husband, Ghazi-ud-din Haidar, get married to the daughter of an English colonel, who was later known as Mubarak Mahal. Badsha Begum was so aggrieved by this act that she managed to have him dismissed. She reappointed Agha Mir, who was desperately trying to win back her confidence. Agha Mir had even approached the begum's personal attendant, Faiz-un-nisa, to help him. This minister, to serve his interest, later created a rift between the begum and her husband. He managed to make her life so difficult that once, on royal order, she was forbidden all services and lived only on food and drinks prepared by either herself or by her granddaughters, Hazi Begum and Wazir Begum.

Badsha Begum retaliated when, after the death of Ghazi-ud-din, her foster-son, Nasir-ud-din Haidar, sat on the throne in the year 1827. Her first act was to get the services of Agha Mir terminated, and in his place appoint her loyal confidant Mir Fazal Ali, who was given the title of 'Etamud-ud-daulah'. It was to Badsha Begum's misfortune that this minister worked only for thirteen months and seven days; he left after this period because of an unpleasant encounter with the king and his friends.

The third minister, in whose ouster she played an important role, was Hakim Mehdi Ali Khan who was appointed on 4 November 1830. This minister tried to curtail the expenses of the begum and even spoke harshly to her servants who were sent to him to collect money. At last Badsha Begum joined hands with other royal ladies and had him thrown out of his job: the king — goaded by the royal women and for his own reasons — sacked Hakim Mehdi Ali on 5 August 1832. After this, Badsha Begum, along with Qudsia

Mahal, helped Roshan-ud-daulah to become the fourth minister of Awadh. Unfortunately, this minister too, because of the politics of the palace, later betrayed her.

Because of her role in the making and unmaking of ministers, she was called Naibgar, or minister-maker, by historians.

Unique Eunuchs of Awadh

The Nawabi era was a golden period for eunuchs in Awadh. They were not only appointed to important administrative posts in the kingdom, but also became so powerful, that often they played a decisive role in the appointment of prime ministers and removal of rulers of Awadh.

Since the beginning of the dynasty, the skills of eunuchs were utitlised. Sadr-i-Jahan, the queen of the second Nawab, Safdar Jung, appointed a eunuch Muharram Ali Khan as Nawab Nazir and entrusted other official duties to eunuchs like Javed Khan, Mian Dana, Mian Bahryab, Bakhtawar and Matbuh Ali Khan. Since Muharram Ali and Matbuh Ali were known to be close confidantes of the queen in matters of money, after her demise, they were arrested by her grandson, the fourth Nawab Asif-ud-daulah, and tortured in order to discover where the late queen had stashed her wealth. According to writer Sheikh Tassaduq Hussain, Asif-ud-daulah later set them free after the confiscation of their assets.

Following the practice of Sadr-i-Jahan, her daughter-in-law Bahu Begum, the wife of Shuja-ud-daulah also trusted eunuchs and recognised their administrative skills. She appointed a eunuch, Jawahar Ali Khan, as the administrative head of around 10,000 employees to manage her estate. Jawahar Ali had the power to appoint workers and terminate the services of inefficient and dishonest employees. He was also given the responsibility of finalising royal leases after Bahu Begum's formal sanction. Impressed by another eunuch, Darab Ali Khan, she appointed him treasurer and gave him the charge of jagirs in the area of Nawabganj and Tanda. Darab Ali Khan and Jawahar Ali Khan had previously worked for Nawab Nazir as well. Unfortunately, Jawahar Ali too was tortured by Nawab Asif-ud-daulah at the time when he was forcing his mother Bahu Begum to give him money. At the same time, another eunuch, Arfin Khan, was playing the most important role of negotiator between Bahu Begum and Asif-ud-daulah.

Perhaps one the most important eunuchs of that period was Almas Ali Khan. Scholar Meer Hassan Ali describes him as a person blessed with a superior mind. Nawab Shuja-ud-daulah's confidante, this eunuch was revenue collector of Mianganj for about forty years. He was so powerful in the court that his personal likes and dislikes could make or mar the career of other important courtiers. His influence was one of the main reasons why Haidar Beg Khan could be appointed as prime minister of Awadh. Apart from this, he was one of the people who conspired with the British to have the fifth nawab Wazir Ali removed from the throne of Awadh. He was given so much importance by the Indian and British both, that George Viscount Valentia, during his visit to Lucknow, went to Almas Ali Khan's house for the breakfast at his invitation, and stayed there long enough to watch a dance performance in his honour.

Almas Ali Khan loved good literature and, like the royals of those days, generously patronised poets. One of the famous poets of Urdu poetry, Insha, was closely associated with him. Insha was so impressed by him, that he wrote a qasida praising Almas Ali Khan.

What's in a Name?

According to historian John Pemble, 'The kings of Oudh were never real kings. Their royalty of the nature of private fantasy was humoured to a limited extent by the British.'

The Nawabs of Lucknow, like rulers all over the world, had a tendency to adopt grandiose titles. For instance, in 1819, the seventh Nawab, Ghazi-ud-din Haidar, declared himself king and adopted two titles: Shah-e-Zaman, meaning 'King of Ages', and Padshah-e-Ghazi, meaning 'Imperial Crusader'. Both titles were rejected by the British.

Shah-e-Zaman was rejected on the grounds that the emperor of Delhi traditionally used it. The British further explained: 'We felt strong objection to any measures which might give colour to a supposition of our concurrence in the elevation of a rival king of India, opposed to the king of Delhi.' Ghazi-ud-din, however, insisted on using the title. At last, the British allowed him to use the title, but with a condition that it was qualified with the rider 'Padshah-e-Awadh', meaning king of Awadh. The Nawab accepted this change in practice, but never on his coins.

The tussle over titles continued even in the time of Ghazi-ud-din's son. In 1827, when Nasir-ud-din Haidar became the king of Awadh, he adopted the title Shah Jahan, meaning 'King of the Universe', which was the name of the fifth Mughal Emperor of India. The British not only sent him a letter stating that they did not approve of the title, they also refused to accept any paper from the Nawab which carried it. Nasir-ud-din Haidar had his title imprinted on coins, but after about two years of objection, this title disappeared from the coinage.

Corruption in Haider's Court

Corruption is one of those weaknesses of mankind which is yet to be overcome, and the officials of Awadhi Lucknow were no exception.

Nawab Nasir-ud-din Haidar, the eighth Nawab, was probably the most visionary ruler of Awadh, but because of the rampant corruption in his administration (historians say that Roshan-ud-daulah — the Nawab's vizier — used to take a five percent bribe for certain deals), none of his projects could actually be implemented.

One of the most remarkable landmarks of Lucknow, the Ghazi-ud-din Haidar canal, is one such project. Nasir-ud-din had named the canal after his father. By this canal he wanted to connect river Ganges flowing at Kanpur with river Gomati at Lucknow. Work on this canal started way back in 1831 with the digging up of land to the depth of forty feet. Unfortunately, the survey and planning was faulty and the people handling this ambitious project were corrupt and incompetent. Understandably, the project could not be completed. A British engineer's services were commissioned in the year 1833 to revive the project, but by this time the funds were exhausted.

If this project had actually gone according to the Nawab's plan, it could have changed the course of Lucknow in terms of trade, commerce and prosperity, as rivers were the major sources of transportation in those days. It would also have been a boon for farmers, as it would have irrigated the land along the line. Nasir-ud-din was clearly a farsighted ruler. Unfortunately, he was hampered by the corruption of his officials.

Clearly, corruption ran through the rank and file of the Nawab's government. Once, the renowned poet, Mirza Ghalib,

Nawab Nasir-ud-din Haidar

sent a Qasida praising Nasir-ud-din Haidar to the Nawab. Nasir-ud-din Haidar liked it so much that he ordered his courtiers to send Ghalib a reward of Rs 5,000. The money never reached the great poet however: the Nawab's courtiers made away with it.

Shia Ulama in Awadh

During the Nawabi era, the Shia Ulama, at times, had greater control over the population of Awadh then the rulers of the realm. The influence they exerted on the masses was so great, that even the king avoided a direct confrontation with them for fear of a general uprising.

An interesting incident from the period of the eighth Nawab and the second king of Awadh, Nasir-ud-din Haider, demonstrates the Ulama's hold on the public.

Nawab Nasir-ud-din Haider did not get along well with the then Mujtahid (Shia jurist), Maulana Syed Mohammad, the elder son of the respected Maulvi Dildar Ali. This was because the Maulana had refused to issue a fatwa in some cases as per the wishes of the king. Apart from this, he refused to meet the king. Nasir-ud-din Haider became so angry, that he issued orders to gun down the house of the Maulana.

On receiving the royal orders, the officer, Nawab Maqbool-ud-daulah, placed one gun facing the residence of the Maulana and mounted another gun pointed towards the palace of the king. Why a gun towards the royal palace?

Writes Syed Mohammad Baqar: 'It was learnt that Maqbool-ud-daulah's faith in religion did not permit him to blow up the residence of the spiritual King [while leaving] the palace of the temporal king...intact.' Understanding the situation, the king had no option but to rescind his orders.

Learned Shia Ulama lived in great style and dignity. According to Agha Mehdi, the word 'Sarkar' was used as a form of address exclusively for the Mujtahids. They generally moved about in palkis (palanquins) equipped with masnads (a kind of pillow), khasdans (betel dish) and the highly ornamental and expensive Muradabadi lotas (copper vessels for drinking water). Touching the feet of the Mujtahids out of respect was very much the done thing. After their death, like the rulers of Awadh, they were given new titles by which they were referred to thereafter.

Shia Ulama, apart from performing religious rituals, played an important role in social life also. For example, at the time of a coronation, it was the Mujtahidul Asr (Shia religious jurist) who placed the crown on the head of a new king. Similarly, they performed marriage and death rituals of the king and his relatives. On special occasions like Id, the king presented the chief priest an elephant as a gift, which generally the chief priest in turn sold off at a throwaway price.

Except Shuja-ud-daulah, almost all the rulers of Awadh were pro-Shia. But it was the reign of the tenth Nawab, Amjad Ali Shah, that saw the pinnacle of Shia Ulama glory; it was at this time that they ruled Awadh both spiritually and temporally. Nawab Amjad Ali was extremely religious and tried to run his government along the dictates of the Shia Ulama. As a result, he introduced such changes in the judicial system which allowed the Shia Ulama to control and run it. He created a new department, Mohakmai Marafai Shari (department for the formulation of religious rules and regulations), headed by the Mujtahidul Asr, Sultan-ul-Ulama, who presided over the highest court of appeal in both the civil and the ecclesiastical cases.

The Mujtahidul Asr also had original jurisdiction in such civil matters like charity, matrimony, registration of documents for mortgage, murder cases and reduction of civil taxes. Sultan ul-Ulema's son, Maulvi Syed Baqar, was posted as Chief of Adalati Alia or the High Court of Judicature. Historian Bhatnagar explains, 'The dominion was divided into the 12 divisions each under a Shia Mufti [who was] paid between Rs 60 and Rs 150. The Adalati Alia heard appeals against these Muftis.'

The tenth Nawab, Amjad Ali Shah

Another department created by Amjad Ali for religious affairs was called Mohakmai Sadrul Shariyat. It gave guidance in the area of Namaz and other tenets of the Shia sect. Shia Maulvi, Syed Mahmmad Hadi, headed it.

According to Safdar Hussain, Amjad Ali had made available funds for zakat or charity by allocating 2.5 percent of the yearly collection of the state revenue, which amounted to around Rs 3 lakh in those days. The Shia chief priest headed the distribution of this fund. The Shia high priest also headed the excise department which enforced prohibition.

Clearly, during Amjad Ali's time, the Shia Ulama were de facto rulers, with a say in the day to day functioning of the government.

The Battle between a Mother and her Son

Of the strained relation between Nasir-ud-din Haidar and his foster mother, Badsha Begum, the famous historian K.S. Santha writes: 'The story of [the] King's petty harassment of his mother is a sordid tale in the history of Awadh'.

Discord between the two had been going on for some time, because of a rift created between them by a minister, Hakim Mehdi. The minister was bent upon reducing Badsha Begum's expenses, which she protested against. To weaken her position, Hakim Mehdi poisoned the mind of Nasir-ud-din and instigated him to disown his own son, Munna Jan, who was being groomed by Badsha Begum as heir apparent. Nasir-ud-din informed the British Resident about his decision and had posters pasted all over city, announcing that Munna Jan had been disinherited. Badsha Begum was not one to take this lying down, and she in turn questioned Nasir-ud-din's legitimacy.

The strained relationship exploded in its ugliest form at the death of the king's favourite wife, Qudsia Begum. The Nawab — ignoring all the administrative matters at the court — declared an unusually long mourning period at her death. He instructed all his courtiers and palace inmates to wear black clothes as a mark of grief. Nasir-ud-din's frequent visits, with all the important persons of the court, to the burial place of Qudsia Mahal, started hampering the proper functioning of the court. He expected his mother too to observe the mourning by dressing in black, but she refused outright. According to *Tarikh-Badsha Begum*, she told her son that no one in the family had mourned the death of even his father, Ghazi-ud-din Haidar, or grandfather Saadat Ali Khan, by dressing in black. She also informed him that his demonstration of grief was being ridiculed in his absence and that it was better for everyone if he focused on his work.

Hurt by Badsha Begum's advice, according to *Sawanihat-i-Salatin-i-Awadh*, Nasir-ud-din started harrowing her with his offensive behaviour. Often they quarrelled on minor issues raised by Nasir-ud-din; his mother generally tried to handle the situation patiently and gracefully. This probably encouraged the Nawab: one day he sent her a letter asking her to leave the palace and settle down in another part of the city, failing which he would confiscate her jagir. Badsha Begum was a strong woman, so she not only refused to vacate the palace, but also argued that it was not his property as her late husband and his father, Nawab Ghazi-ud-din Haidar, had given it to her. She also threatened him that if he did not desist from such acts, she would report the matter to the British Government. The Nawab did not take this threat seriously because he was sure that the British would be on his side. On this assumption, the Nawab asked the British Resident posted at Lucknow to intervene on his behalf, but the Resident refused, saying it was the Nawab's domestic affair. When the Nawab saw that things were not working out in his favour, he decided to try another tactic.

The Nawab decided to make her life miserable in the palace. He instructed a group of labourers engaged in the maintenance and the construction of buildings for the royals, to go to her quarters, without taking her customary permission. They were told to stand at those points from were they could clearly see into the inner parts of her apartment and watch the movements of the inmates, thus violating her privacy. When these measures proved ineffective, his men were asked to throw earthen pots containing stinking garbage, urine and offal inside her place. Unfortunately, the garbage and other detritus fell on the tombs of the twelve Imams also, and the helpless begum, assisted by maidservants, had to clear it herself.

The Nawab also blocked the passage that connected her apartments with the palace, thus she was left with only one exit that opened on the market side. He even stopped the supply of food to her and her staff. When every other thing failed he tried, through his staff and the British, to convince her to take a monthly salary of Rs 25,000 and leave the palace.

Finally, in 1835, there was an armed clash between the staff of mother and son in which she lost her four slave girls and was pushed out of the palace.

Once out of the palace, Badsha Begum decided to live at Almas Bagh, and started consolidating her position by recruiting armed personnel. Soon there was another big showdown between her and the king's armed men. This time her side proved to be so powerful that Nasir-ud-din had to take the help of the British to save the situation. At the end, the British pressurised Badsha Begum to withdraw her forces.

The Fight to Keep Awadh

The tenth Nawab of Awadh, Amjad Ali Shah, was the most religious of all the Nawabs. He ascended the throne in 1842, at the age of forty-one, and will always be remembered for establishing the upscale market, Hazratganj, in Lucknow.

His chief consort, Malika Kishwar Taj Ara Begum, was from the famous Delhi-based Khan-i-Khana family. She was not only courageous and beautiful, but also very practical. Although she did not play any significant political role during the reign of her husband, her son, Nawab Wajid Ali Shah, according to writer Najmul Ghani Rampuri, sought her advice on crucial issues related to the interests of the kingdom, and when appointing high-ranking officials in court.

The British did not like this and asked the king to stop her from interfering in administrative affairs. Still, this did not prevent the British Resident, Col. Sleeman, from recommending her name for the Regency Council of Awadh. He was so impressed with her acumen, statesmanship and foresight that, Safi Ahmed records, her name was one of the first to be proposed to the Council.

Legend goes that Malika Kishwar was dressing up after her bath when she was informed that the British had annexed the kingdom of Awadh.

She was so shocked by this news that, uncharacteristically for her, she rushed out barefooted and bareheaded. Shouting, 'The kingdom is destroyed!' she reached Wajid Ali's parlour. Face-to-face with the Nawab, according to William Knighton, she asked, 'Are you now satisfied? Have you got at last the wages of your dancing, your singing and your fiddling? Have I not often told you that it would come to this?'

Once calmed down, and realising the changed circumstances, the begum decided not to give up. She, in consultation with her son Wajid Ali and other important persons, went to England in 1856 with the Crown Prince Mirza Hamid Ali, her younger son, Prince Sikander Hashmat, courtier Masihuddin Khan, and a few others, to plead against this injustice. She met Queen Victoria at Buckingham Palace on 4 July 1857, but her mission failed.

Disappointed, but wanting to make the best of things, she applied for a pension to the Court of Directors. The begum also asked for a three-lakh rupee advance so she could go to Kaaba on a pilgrimage. Unfortunately, her request was turned down, and she died on her way back to India, in Paris.

This devout Shia begum was fond of studying religious books. According to Sheik Tassaduq Hussain, in the morning a maulvi, who sat on the other side of a curtain, recited the Holy Quran in her presence. On the tenth day of Muharram, the begum, along with other family members, observed a fast. She was so particular about rituals that even babies were not provided milk till the time Tazias were buried.

Social causes were very close to her heart, especially those concerning women. Knighton records that she held darbar to hear grievances of women from all over the kingdom. Unluckily, her servants allowed them to have audience with her only when their palms had been greased.

Was Amjad Ali's Minister a Spy?

History is one of the very few subjects which is coloured so deeply by the likes and the dislikes of its practitioner. The resultant subjectivity with regard to a person or an event means that a reader may never know the entire truth.

The same is true in the case of Imdad Hussain Khan Amin-ud-daulah, the founder of the famous market, Aminabad, which he established while serving as a minister to the tenth king, Amjad Ali Shah, who ruled Awadh between 17 May 1842 and 13 February 1847.

While a good number of historians project Amin-ud-daulah as an ideal administrator and a god-fearing man, others have a view that is diametrically opposite. According to them, he was an incompetent person and an opium addict. They also accuse him of being a British spy in the court of Awadh. When Mir Mehadi, a courtier of Wajid Ali Shah, started dismantling temples, Hindu jewellers took a procession to the Resident to complain about this provocative act. However, the Resident did not intervene, apparently because one of Amin-ud-daulah's men, Gulab Rai, was also involved in damaging the temples. M. Najmul Ghani Rampuri, author of *Tareekh-e-Awadh*, records, 'This clearly proves that Amin-ud-daulah was the protégé of the Resident.'

Prime Minister Amin-ud-daulah

According to Lord Hasting's Dispatch No. 33, dated 2 December 1847, 'Mr Davidson reported on the 29th May 1846, that [the] minister was quite unfit for his office — that he could neither read nor write, and he, being an opium eater, was disqualified for several hours of each day for transacting public business.'

On 9 July 1847, when the same minister was removed from his post after he was assaulted in a street in broad daylight in April 1847, the Resident, Colonel Richmond, tried to reinstate him. However, the new king, Wajid Ali, refused. According to writer and historian Mirza Ali Azhar, '[the] British Resident, Richmond, was interested in Amin-ud-daulah because he was the Resident's spy on the King and entirely in his grip.'

Palace to Rented House

There are very few rulers in history who experienced such vicissitudes of life as did King Wajid Ali Shah. When the British took over the kingdom of Awadh and unceremoniously divested Wajid Ali Shah of his crown and throne, he decided to plead his case and expose the Company's conduct to the British public.

For this purpose he left Lucknow on 13 March 1856 at around 8 p.m. Apart from about 300 persons from the court, his retinue included his wives Maashuq Mahal and Nawab Khas Mahal, the Queen Mother; his brother Mirza Sikander Hashmat; Raja Yusuf Ali Khan, Munshi Meer Baqar Ali Khan, Hakim Meer Mohammad Ali, Major Bird; the heir apparent, Nawab Munawwar-ud-daulah; and Amjad Ali Khan. In the coach box of the royal carriage sat an English businessman from Kanpur, Brandon, and Ahsan-ud-daulah and Bashir-ud-daulah rode the horses.

The British Resident, Colonel James Outram, who was instrumental in the annexation of the kingdom, tried every trick to break the deposed king's spirit and morale that he may never recoup his lost powers and dare challenge the British authority in Awadh. Outram gave orders to the staff of the secretariat, Bait-ul-Insh, and Munshi-Khana not to go along with Wajid Ali. Not only this, Outram also seized the carriage-horses of the former king and arrested twenty-one members of his personal staff. In his next move, Outram and his officials seized all the official documents and public records that Wajid Ali would need to plead his case. The Resident even prevented the prime minister, Syed Ali Naqi Khan, the finance minister Raja Balkrishna and the government record keeper, Baboo Puran Chand, from accompanying Wajid Ali. He also placed many other officers loyal to the king under surveillance.

King Wajid Ali Shah

On his way to Calcutta, Wajid Ali reached Kanpur on 14 March 1856 and remained there for twenty-four days. It was here that the Maharaja of Banaras, Ishri Prasad Singh, sent an invitation to him through Nawab Munawwar-ud-daulah to stay as his guest at Benaras. This invitation was accepted. Wajid Ali left Kanpur on 7 April, and after spending eight days at Allahabad, he reached Benaras on 16 April.

At Benaras, Wajid Ali enjoyed the hospitality of the Maharaja of Banaras for ten days. The Maharaja considered rulers of Awadh as traditional allies. Wajid Ali was so moved by the Maharaja's treatment that he visited his capital Ramnagar. From there he once again set out for Calcutta via the river Ganges. Finally, after two months of leaving the Chattar Manzil palace of Lucknow, Wajid Ali Shah reached Calcutta on 13 May 1856. And ironically, he had no option but to stay in a rented kothi owned by Maharaja of Burdwan that had been arranged in advance by his royal envoy, Maulvi Masih-ud-daulah, on a rent of Rs 2,000 per month.

The Nawab who didn't Dance

It is ironical that Nawab Wajid Ali Shah, who wrote a book on regulations and management, *Dastoor-e-Wajidi*, lost his own kingdom on grounds of mismanagement.

There are two schools of thought with regard to Wajid Ali Shah: British historians paint him as debauched, wasting his time in the company of women, music and dance while ignoring the administration and the welfare of his subjects. Colonel W.H. Sleeman — the British Resident between 1849 and 1856 and the author of *A Journey through the Kingdom of Oudh* — belongs to this school.

On the other hand, native historians, like Mirza Ali Azhar, Abdul Haleem Sharar and others, refute these charges and have tried to establish that it was part of a campaign on the part of the British to tarnish Wajid Ali's reputation; this gave them an excuse to annex Awadh on the pretext of the king's inefficiency. According to Azhar, the British tried to take advantage of Islam's animus against dancing. He writes, 'The King, it is said, used to dance, but it is absolutely wrong and baseless.' According to him, 'Many paintings, which depict him dancing surrounded by his Mahals [wives], were spread all over the country. But after making searching inquiries I came to know that they were all fake.'

Sharar, in *Jan-e-Alam*, agrees. 'The fact is he never danced, not even when he was the king at Lucknow nor in Matia Burj. But being expert in music and having watched dance intensively, he had acquired an insight in the intricacies of the art so much that if any mistake was committed in dancing, the King would point it out while sitting on his Palang [bed] and gave the correct direction by raising both his hands and saying: "not that way but this way".'

It was these postures that the British used as evidence to prove that Nawab Wajid Ali danced, it is argued.

The Truth behind the Nawab's Marriage

It was in June 1851, with a dowry of Rs 25 lakhs, that Nawab Wajid Ali Shah married Raunaq Ara Begum, the third daughter of the Nawab's minister Ali Naqi Khan. Wajid Ali was then twenty-nine, and the begum, eleven years old. While some writers opine that Wajid Ali married Raunaq Ara Begum because of her considerable charms (Tassadduq Hussain, for example, says, that Raunaq Ara Begum was well known for her musical voice and beauty and Wajid Ali Shah was a connoisseur of music, which brought them closer), a letter from Col. W.H. Sleeman to Lord Dalhousie tells a different story.

According to Col. W.H. Sleeman, the Nawab married her in order to save his life. In a letter to Lord Dalhousie, dated 11 November 1853, Sleeman writes, 'The minister has by his intrigues put himself so much in power that he [the king] dare not do anything to offend him. The man can at once ruin him by his exposures if he found it necessary for his own security. The King to save himself married one of the minister's pretty daughters.

'...The king's chief consort was the niece of the minister, and her son, the heir apparent, so it was in her interest, and that of her uncle, for the minister to get rid of the king. The king's mother is supposed to have given him a hint of the danger. He took liking to one of the daughters and married her in order to make it the minister's interest to keep him alive.'

How the Nawabs were used as Pawns

It is interesting to note that the Nawabs of Awadh — who had complete power over their subjects — were, in fact, themselves controlled by the British like pawns in the game of power and politics. Depending on what was in their best interests, the British were installing, toppling or having Nawabs killed.

Nawab Wazir Ali operated too independently for the Britishers' tastes. As a result, he was called to Lucknow, purportedly for a meeting, arrested there and sent to Varanasi. The British then brought his uncle, Saadat Ali Khan, from Varanasi and installed him on the throne of Awadh. This they did in exchange of almost half the kingdom, which generated a revenue of about one crore thirty five lakh rupees a year.

Saadat Ali had chosen to groom his son Ghazi-ud-din Haider, who was known at that time as Raffut-ud-daulah, as the heir apparent. However, British officers, with their ulterior motives, manipulated the courtiers and inmates of the palace in such a way that father and son eventually drifted apart. At one point of time, Ghazi-ud-din was ready to revolt against his father, which is why Saadat Ali held him under house arrest. After the death of his father, when he was set free, Ghazi-ud-din approached the British with the recommendation of minister Mirza Zafar. He assured them that if he were made the ruler, he would always be loyal to them. The British decided to install him on the throne, a decision that paid off right from the beginning: Ghazi-ud-din, on his installation, gifted one crore rupees to Governor-General Hastings.

When Ghazi-ud-din died on 18 October 1827, Nasir-ud-din Haider became the ruler of Awadh. The British did not take a liking to him, and started to portray him in bad taste. The East India Company considered annexing the company, but the Board of Directors did not agree at this time. When the Nawab died from poisoning in 1837, the British, once again out of turn, installed Mohammad Ali Shah on the throne, ignoring the violent resistance of others.

Nawab Saadat Ali Khan

It said that the last Nawab, Wajid Ali Shah, could not even shift his throne from one room to another without the permission of the British Resident.

The rulers of Awadh, for the most part, were evidently mere pawns.

Legal Action against the King

It is difficult to believe that King Wajid Ali Shah, who himself decided the fate of millions and whose judgement made or marred the fortunes of the richest of his state, would one day be at the mercy of someone else to decide his case like a common man.

When, after the annexation of his kingdom, Wajid Ali was living at Matia Burj in Calcutta on a yearly pension of Rs 12 lakh, his money was misappropriated by one of his most trusted officials, Munshi Safdar.

This man had managed to win Wajid Ali's confidence to such a degree that the king not only made him the in-charge of construction and maintenance of all the palaces, parks and royal gardens, but also honoured him with the titles of 'Lisan-ul-Mulk' and 'Mahmud-ud-daulah'.

Munshi Safdar, along with other employees, debited the king's account with false expenses and this fraudulent practice was not detected in his lifetime. After his death it was discovered that, as per Munshi Safdar's manipulated accounts, the king owed others about a crore of rupees.

According to these fictitious accounts, the king had to give Rs 42 lakhs to Munshi Safdar's family. Ali Khan records in his famous book *Wazeernamah*, that Munshi Safdar's son-in-law Turab Ali filed a suit against the Nawab in Calcutta, in order to recover the amount. The king engaged the then leading lawyer of Bengal, Syed Amir Ali Khan Bhadur of the Sudder Dewani Adalat.

Act XIII of 1868 exempted King Wajid Ali Shah from the jurisdiction of Criminal and Civil Courts, so he was issued thirty-six interrogatories that the king had to reply to himself as no Counsel was allowed to cross-examine the king. It took nine days for the king to write the reply in the presence of the Agent to the Governor General, Col. Herbert, and his Mir Munshi, Maulvi Fateh Ali.

At the end of this legal battle, the total payable amount came down to Rs 7 lakhs, and was payable in instalments.

A Palace is turned into a Kennel

At the zenith of the Nawabi age, when Nawabs ruled their kingdom sitting on a jewel-studded throne in the magnificent palace, Farah Bukhsh, near Chattar Manzil, no one could have imagined that one day, in the very same palace, only dogs would live.

After usurping Awadh on 7 February 1856, the British started eliminating signs of Nawab Wajid Ali's authority. According to Mirja Ali Azhar in *King Wajid Ali Shah of Awadh*, on 4 March 1856, the officials at Lucknow were directed to execute the 'sale by public auction [of] the entire stud and other animals belonging to [the] ex-King'. And, on 17 March, the Deputy Commissioner was issued orders, 'that the whole of the livestock reserved for the ex-King or otherwise be brought to the hammer on the 20 March'.

The Deputy Commissioner, Simpson, and City Magistrate of Lucknow, Carnegie, first levelled down Jilau-Khana near Baillie Guard. According to S. Kamaluddin Haidar, in *Qaisar-ut-Tawareekh*, both the gates of Hazratganj, belonging to Nawab Mulka, were demolished to widen the highway; the Dowlut-khana of Asif-ud-daulah was converted into barracks for European soldiers; the king's elephant stable was converted into a hospital.

Wajid Ali gave details of the destruction in a letter dated 30 August 1856 to Lord Canning stating that thousands of his effects had been confiscated and destroyed, and that monuments and a building which had cost lakhs of rupees had been pulled down. Further in the letter he says the doors of his godown were broken and its goods destroyed. The animals, such as horses, elephant and bullocks, were sold by auction.

In other letters he informs that his entire collection of books was removed to La Martinere College, valuable arms were sold by auction, his begums' pin money was stopped and his family forcefully dragged out from Chattar Manzil Palace.

Finally he writes: 'The magnificent building, Farah Bukhsh, in which the throne is placed, [is being] used as [a] dog kennel.'

And thus, vanished the golden age of the Nawabs.

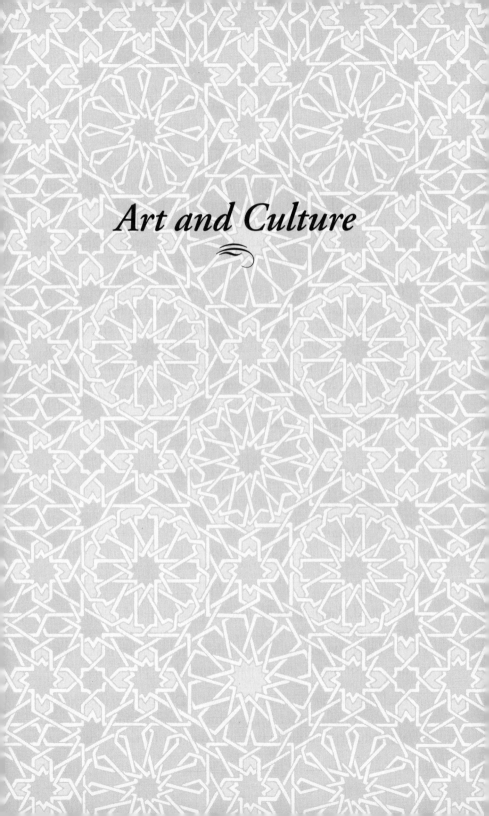

Art and Culture

Delhi's Loss is Lucknow's Gain

Lucknow's contribution to Urdu literature and poetry is significant. It would not be an exaggeration to say that Awadh, and particularly Lucknow, was the capital of Urdu. Nawabi culture was so tailor-made and conducive for Urdu poetry that it reached greater heights in Awadh than its place of origin, the Deccan, or the place of its further development, Delhi.

The reason for this, was the typical twists and turns of politics. With the gradual loss of power, the Mughal emperors could not afford to financially patronise poets in their Delhi courts. As a result, these poets, who were traditionally dependent on the support of the court, were on the verge of starvation. According to the legendary poet, Mir Taqui Mir, when he wanted to leave Delhi for Lucknow, he did not even have enough money for the journey. Another famous poet, Sauda, in his renowned poem *Shahr-e Ashob*, depicted in detail the poverty of Delhi. He writes:

> *...There is no house where jackals don't howl.*
>
> *If one goes to a mosque for*
>
> *Evening prayers*
>
> *He will find no lamp except the lamp of darkness...*

The splinter states of the Mughal Empire, like Hyderabad, Murshidabad, Arcot, Farrukhabad, Rohilkhand and Awadh, were, however, financially well placed. And the rulers of these states, who had to some extent acquired the tastes of their masters, and for the sake of status, started patronising these poets.

Lucknow was geographically closer to Delhi, and was backed by the British; Awadh, therefore, presented a more politically peaceful picture and attracted the maximum number of poets. Apart from the affluence of the state — generated from agricultural revenue — the Nawabi culture was an additional attraction for the migrant-poet.

Initially, the poets of Delhi were reluctant to leave their city, but faced with the prospect of a bleak future in that city, and the tempting offers made by the Nawabs at Lucknow, they soon changed their mind. Sauda, too, at first rejected Nawab Shuja-ud-daulah's offer, but later joined the court at Faizabad in 1771. He moved to Lucknow when it was being ruled by Nawab Asif-ud-daulah. The Nawab gave him a salary of Rs 6,000 a year and the title 'Malik-ush-Shaura' or Poet Laureate. Sauda is especially recognised for his contribution to the Qasida and Hajo style of poetry: the first is laudatory in nature, and the second is satirical.

But the first prominent poet to join Awadh was Mir Siraj-ud-din Khan Arzoo, who joined the court around 1754. He unfortunately died just two years later. Urdu writer and critic Dr Abullais Siddiqui, in his *Lakhnau Ka Dabistan-e-Shairi*, says Arzoo was buried in Delhi as per his own wishes.

Mir Taqui Mir, regarded by author R.B. Saxena as the Sheik Saadi of Urdu ghazals, was so disappointed by the conditions prevailing in Delhi that, despite repeated invitations by the Emperor Alamgir the Second, he did not present himself at the 'beggarly' court.

According to *Khuda-e-Sukhan*, written by Idrees Siddiqui, Mir Taqui Mir reached Lucknow in 1782. Saxena, in his *A History of Urdu Literature*, says he was introduced to Nawab Asif-ud-daulah at a cockfight, and soon thereafter, he was given employment.

Although Mir lived in Lucknow for almost twenty-six years, and it was there that his poetry flourished, giving him a prestigious place in the annals of Urdu poetry, Abdullah Yusuf Ali says in his work, *Angrezi Ahad Mein Hindustan ke Tamaddum ki Tarikh*, that despite the recognition Mir received in Lucknow, he could not reconcile himself to the city's lifestyle. Mir opens up his heart when he says:

Ten times better than Lucknow was Delhi's devastation

I wish I had died there and had not come here in desperation.

While in Lucknow, Mir initially lived in the area known as Muftiganj; he later shifted to the Imambara of Mian Almas Ali Khan on Kakori Road.

Apart from these well-established masters of poetry, over a period of time many other talented poets also migrated from Delhi to Lucknow. Notable amongst them are Ashraf Ali Khan Fughan, renowned for his harmonic combinations of Hindi and Persian idioms; Nasim Dehlavi; Meer Hasan, famous for his masnawi *Sihr-ul-Bayan*; Saadat Yar Rangin; Meer Matah Khaleeq; Ghulam Hamdani Musahfi; Mir Qamruddin Minnat; Meer Zia-uddin Zia; Mirza Zafar Ali Hasarat; Meer Inshaullah Khan Insha; Meer Haider Ali Hairan; and Qalander Bux Jurat. It is said that Mirza Ghalib too stayed in Lucknow on his way to Calcutta.

Although Lucknow too had produced its own poets, like Imam Bux Nasikh and Atish, who were born in Faizabad, by and large the poetry — which later came to be known as the 'Lucknow School' — was evolved by the migrant poets from Delhi. Clearly, Delhi's loss was Lucknow's gain.

Poet Sauda

The Palace of Learning

In Mughal times, Lucknow was an important trading centre. Once, attracted by the business prospects, a French horse trader established a stable in the city. In the very first year he earned so much profit that he built four beautiful houses near Chowk; the houses were popularly known as Firangi Mahal because of its European owner. Unfortunately, the state did not extend the horse trader's stay and he was forced to leave Lucknow; Firangi Mahal was confiscated.

In those days, the important centres of Islamic studies were located at Lucknow, Kakori, Malihabad, Sandila and Bilgram in Hardoi, Nasirabad and Jais in Rae Bareilly and Rudauli and Kichhocha in Faizabad district. The courses offered in these institutes were based on the Hanafi version of education and the subjects available were Hadis (sayings of the Prophet), Fikah (jurisprudence) and Tafseer (interpretation of Quran).

The turning point in Islamic studies came when Emperor Aurangzeb presented Firangi Mahal to Mulla Saeed, a native of Sahali in Barabanki, who had shifted to Lucknow after his father, Mulla Qutub Uddin, was murdered by the Sheikzades of Painitpur. Mulla Saeed's scholar son, Mulla Nizamuddin, started a school here and the Firangi Mahal was renamed as the Farhangi Mahal, or the palace of learning.

Soon, Mulla Nizamuddin made it a renowned centre of learning. The syllabus prepared by him, known as Silsila-e-Nizamia, was accepted as a standard, not only in India, but across Asia. Apart from religion, fundamentals of grammar, literature, logic, philosophy and metaphysics were also taught here.

The scholars of this institute, who served in the Awadh government, were Maulvi Zaheer Ullah, who was a Mufti-e-Adalat (religious judge) for forty years; Maulvi Wali Ullah, who served as senior officer to the Nawab; Maulvi Abdulwali; and Abdul Razaq. Many renowned Shia Ulama, like Maulvi Dildar Ali, were also the products of this Sunni-sect school.

The First Institute of Shia Theology

Before Nawab Amjad Ali Shah, who ascended the throne at the age of forty-one in 1842, there was no organised school of Shia theology in Awadh. Shia boys and Ulama used to study in the world-renowned school of Sunni theology at Farhangi Mahal.

Even the legendary Shia Ulama, Maulvi Dildar Ali, had no choice but to study in this Sunni school. It was Amjad Ali who met this long-standing requirement of the Shias. This Nawab, according to different historians, had a religious bent of mind and this manifested in his administration.

Amjad Ali established an exclusive school of Shia theology in the mausoleum of Nawab Saadat Ali Khan at Lucknow and named it Madarsai Sultania, which means Royal College. It was later shifted and accommodated in the famous Asifi Imambara. Its organisational set-up was such, that its management remained in the hands of Mujtahidul Asr, Islamic scholars / priests with expertise in a particular branch of religion. His nephew, Maulana Syed Mohammad Taqi, was appointed the principal of the college. The salary of teachers varied as per their qualification and ranged between Rs 20 and Rs 100 per month.

Students of this college received financial assistance between Rs 4 and Rs 9, depending on their level of learning.

Historian G.D. Bhatnagar writes in his book *Awadh under Wajid Ali Shah*, 'This school had a boarding house consisting [of] ten rooms, under the charge of Mufti Mir Mohammad Abbas.' Another learned historian, Agha Mehdi, mentions in his book, *Tarikh-i-Lucknow*, that 'the total expenses on this institute amounted to Rs 2,600 per month.' Unfortunately, the British closed down this historical institute after annexing Awadh.

Underground Poetry Sittings in Lucknow

One of the many manifestations of Shia influence on the Awadhi way of life, was a form of poetry, known as harsiya. In this form of poetry, Shias ridiculed a few Khalifas of Islam, which the Sunnis resented. It was because of this, that most harsiya poetry remained unpublished and underground. Poetry reading sessions were also in exclusively underground sittings.

One of the popular harsiya writers of that time, Mian Mushir, was a pupil of the renowned poet, Dabir. Mian Mushir was regularly invited to annual underground sittings that were organised in the Mohalla Pir Bukhara on the last Sunday of Rabi-ul-Awwal. The sittings were discontinued in 1857, but were started again after a lapse of six years.

It is interesting to note that there was another kind of poetry too, also unpublished and underground. According to author Agha Mehadi, the nobility held underground mushairas at which vulgar and obscene verses were freely recited. The popular names associated with this genre of poetry were Sahib Qaran, Jan Sahib and Chirkin.

In the Nawabi era, mushairas and poetry were essential parts of the culture of Lucknow. Even opium addicts were not untouched by this. In *Qadeem Lakhnaw Aj Kal*, Mirja Jaffar Hussain narrates: 'The opium addicts of the whole city used to gather and recite verses [at a] fair [known as] Tar, held on the day following Eid at Aish Bagh.'

Schools of Art in Awadh

During the reign of Nawab Shuja-ud-daulah, two styles of miniature paintings developed. One is referred to as the Later Provincial Mughal School of Lucknow, and the other as Raga Mala. The first was adopted to paint the lifestyle of the affluent side of Awadh and Lucknow, and the latter was used to depict nature and human emotions. Both these styles remained the main medium of expression till the time of Nawab Shuja-ud-daulah's son Asif-ud-daulah. However, local art was also influenced by visiting English artists.

Nawab Shuja-ud-daulah invited renowned English artist Tilly Kettle to Faizabad to paint his six portraits. After Tilly Kettle, John Zoffany, in 1784, and Ozias Humphry, in 1786, painted for Nawab Asif-ud-daulah.

Nawab Ghazi-ud-din Haidar also had a European artist, Robert Home, in his court. The European artist who probably painted the most number of Nawabs, is John Beechey. He painted portraits of Nawab Nasir-ud-din Haidar, Nawab Mohammad Ali Shah, Nawab Amjad Ali Shah and Nawab Wajid Ali Shah after he came to Lucknow in 1828 during the time of Nasir-ud-din. He lived in Lucknow till his death in 1852.

The work of these European painters started influencing local artists, sometimes at the insistence of the customer. As European artists and their work was being patronised by the Nawabs, other customers began insisting that the same kind of work and style be produced from local artists.

Later on, when the British started dominating the scene, artists began to paint their lifestyle, customs and other events connected with their presence in India. This style was termed as the 'Company style'. Artist Mummoo Jan is considered as one of the most important artists of this phase.

Popularisation of Classical Music

Lucknow, especially Nawab Wajid Ali Shah, has been credited with popularising classical North Indian music, helping it emerge from a select circle of admirers and practitioners to a wider audience. Music became so popular in Lucknow that it was common to find even street urchins singing ragas in such perfect melody that anyone could have taken them for trained singers.

Music was always an intrinsic part of Awadh: several of its cities, such as Benaras, Jaunpur and Ayodhya, were centres of musical training. In the Nawabi era, at the time of the third Nawab, Shuja-ud-daulah, singers from all over the country and even from Tansen's lineage, migrated from Delhi and started making their presence felt in Lucknow. Later, during the reign of Shuja-ud-daulah's son, Asif-ud-daulah, music attained greater heights; the renowned book *Usul un Naghmat ul Asafiya* (The Principle of the Melodies of Asaf) was brought out at this time. The sixth Nawab, Saadat Ali Khan, did not give much importance to music, and, as a result, musicians were unable to do well at this time.

During Ghazi-ud-din Haidar's time, the renowned singer Haidar Khan lived in Golaganj. Because of his whimsical nature he was called 'Cynical Haidary'.

Music did not thrive during the reigns of the ninth Nawab, Mohammad Ali Shah, and the tenth Nawab, Amjad Ali Shah. It was the last king of Awadh, Nawab Wajid Ali Shah, who popularised music in Lucknow. Wajid Ali Shah was musically talented himself. Trained under the renowned Ustad Basit Khan, Wajid Ali composed raginis, like juhi, jogi and Shah Pasand, meaning 'king's favourite'. Wajid Ali was so musically adept, that he composed a thumri by the name 'Kadar Piya' (mean lover).

In Wajid Ali's time, complicated ragas like hori and dhrupad were ignored and easier raginis, like tilak, pilu, sendura, khammach, bhairvi and jhanjhauti were encouraged. As these were liked by the king and easily understood by all sections of society, they came to be well-loved by commoners. It was because of this reason that Lucknow's bhairvi, which is sung in the morning, became a favourite all over the country.

Wajid Ali has been accused of cheapening the classical tradition and promoting lighter forms of music such as ghazals and thumris. But then, this is how popular music has always been criticised.

The Eccentric Singer of Lucknow

The famous classical singer, Haidar Khan, lived in Golaganj. This area was known as Golaganj because there was an ammunition depot in the vicinity ('gola' means cannonball).

Haidar was an artiste in the truest sense. He was always lost in the world of music and completely unaware of what was around him. This sometimes created comical situations as a result of which people popularly called him Sidi Haidary or Cynical Haidary. Nawab Ghazi-ud-din, who ruled Awadh between 1814–1827, was always eager to listen to Haidar sing, but somehow it could not be arranged because of the singer's whimsical nature.

Once, as the evening was mellowing and the Nawab was enjoying a ride along the banks of the River Gomati, his courtiers spotted Haidary near Roomi Gate. The king immediately summoned him and asked, 'Friend Haidary, would you ever sing for me?' Haidary shot back innocently, 'Of course I will sing for you, but I do not know your house.' Ghazi-ud-din smiled at his ignorance and said, 'Fine, come with me, I will show you my house.' The singer went along with him.

As they were approaching Chattar Manzil, the singer became moody and told the king, 'Look, I am coming along with you, but unless I am given poori and balai to eat I will not sing.' The amused Nawab promised to treat Haidary to whatever he wished. Once at the palace, the genius started singing his melodious compositions so well that the Nawab almost went into a trance. But then, Haidary suddenly stopped singing. When the Nawab requested that he continue, Haidary asked, 'The tobacco that you are smoking in your hookah is very good. From which shop did you buy it?' On the advice of the Nawab, Haidary was taken to another room where he was provided a hookah to smoke and given one pav poori and half pav balai with sugar worth one paisa which he demanded be sent to his wife.

When Haidary had eaten, the Nawab sent for him. Just as the artiste began singing, the Nawab himself interrupted him and warned him, 'Listen Haidary, ensure that you not merely entertain me, but make me so happy that I cry in ecstasy. And if you fail, you will be thrown into the Gomati.'

Now for the first time a shocked Haidary realised that he was in front of a Sovereign. Driven by survival instinct he sang to the best of his ability. And luck too was on his side, for as everyone present there listened spellbound, the king began crying in sheer pleasure.

Pleased, the Nawab told Haidary he could ask for anything in reward. Like a child, Haidary asked the Nawab thrice: 'Your Honour, are you sure you will grant me whatever I want?' When the Nawab had assured him that he would, Haidary said: 'Sir, never ask me to come and sing for you again.' A puzzled Ghazi-ud-din asked him why. Haidary replied, 'Your Honour, you are a king. I never know when you might have me killed. And if you die, someone else will be made the king immediately, but if I am dead, then a Haidary will not be born again.' And with this Haidary ran away from the court.

The Artist who refused to sing for the Nawab

In the days of Nawab Saadat Ali Khan, there lived a famous musician and sozkhwan, Meer Ali, in Lucknow. Sozkhwani is the art of reciting elegies in melody. Meer Ali was the pupil of one of the greatest singers of that time, Haideri Khan.

Meer Ali belonged to a noble family, the Syeds, and his contribution to the promotion of sozkhwani is considerable. He had developed his own style of singing, for which he became very popular. He was a much sought after artist and people did not mind waiting hours together to watch one of his performances. Like his legendary Ustad, Haideri Khan, Meer Ali too was a very self-respecting musician and proud of his art. Meer Ali did not only learn the finer points of his art from his mentor, but also the art of living a life of dignity. He was always wary of official patronage for his talent.

When his fame spread, the ruling Nawab Saadat Ali Khan sent him an invitation to come to the royal chamber. Any other musician in his place would have been grateful for this opportunity, but the maverick Meer Ali declined the Nawab's offer with the reply, 'If he is a ruler, I too am a prince. Why should he not come to me?'

Meer Ali was an intelligent person. He knew well the consequences of saying no to the Nawab. To avoid any trouble, he decided to shift to the Deccan. But Mohammad Husain Azad writes in his book, *Aabe Hayat*, that the famous poet, Meer Insha Ullah Khan 'Insha', handled the matter tactfully and prevented embarrassment on both sides. The Nawab ultimately presented Meer Ali with a robe of honour and fixed a monthly payment of Rs 200 per month for him from the court.

Poets and Politics

After the decline of Mughal power in Delhi, splinter states, like Awadh, Furrukhabad, Rohilkhand, Murshidabad and Hyderabad, started flourishing. And, in imitation of the lifestyle of their ex-masters, they patronised anything 'made in Delhi'. Awadh, being closer to Delhi, was more successful in luring poets like Mir Siraj-ud-din Khan 'Arzoo'; he was the first major poet of Delhi who joined the court of Awadh at Faizabad. The poet Sauda, who at first turned down Nawab Shuja-ud-daulah's offer to join his court, later came to Awadh in the year 1771. Similarly, the famous poet, Mir Taqui Mir, joined the Awadh darbar in 1784.

Although it would not be untrue to say that the foundation of Lucknow's Urdu poetry was laid by the poets who migrated from Delhi, it does not mean that Awadh did not produce any poets of its own.

Imam Bakhsh 'Nasikh', the first non-Delhi poet, was the founder of the Lucknow School of Poetry. He was born in Faizabad into an ordinary family. This talented poet, at the early stages of his career, joined the darbar of Nawab Mohammad Taqui Khan, a noble of Faizabad. But his talent required a wider canvas, and so he came to Lucknow and not only continued his education, but also sought the patronage of Meer Kazim Ali, from whom he later inherited some property.

Poets needed to ingratiate themselves with their masters in order to get patronage, so Nasikh, to please Prime Minister Agha Mir, wrote a poem in the hajo style decrying his political rival Hakim Mehdi Ali Khan. Nasikh was rewarded adequately for this. Unfortunately, the poem eventually proved to be a costly exercise, for in 1830, Nawab Nasir-ud-din Haider appointed Hakim Mehdi as prime minister of Awadh. In this changed political situation, the poet had no option but to flee from Lucknow. However, just two years later, in 1832, Hakim Mehdi was sacked from his post and Nasikh returned to Lucknow.

This 'comeback' of the poet was very short-lived, for in 1837, the ninth Nawab, Mohammad Ali Shaw, again brought Hakim Mehdi in power. Again, Nasikh left  Lucknow in a huff and moved to a safer place. This time though, Nasikh did not have to live in exile for long: within a few months of Nasikh's exile, in December 1837, Hakim Mehdi died. Nasikh returned to Lucknow, but he could not enjoy this peace for long: in 1839, Nasikh breathed his last.

Poet Nasikh, co-founder of Lucknow School of Poetry

Mirza Ghalib Joins a Debate

Since the Nawabs of Awadh were Shias, under their rule, for the first time, Shias openly started asserting their identity. They even contested Sunni principles. This public debate between the Shia–Sunni sects was known as Munazira.

According to journalist Abdul Halim Sharar, this debate between the Shias and Sunnis started when Qazi Nur Ullah Shustri of Iran came to India and challenged certain interpretations of Islam by Sunnis. In reaction to this, Shah Abdul Aziz Muhaddis of Delhi refuted Shia precepts. The legendary Maulvi Dildar Ali, who is given the credit of organising the Shias of Lucknow and standardising their rituals, responded to this by writing three books, *Swarumul Al Hayaat*, *Risal-e-Ghibat* and *Hassmul Islam*, defending Shia interpretations.

Maulana Haider Ali, who was settled in Lucknow, also wrote a book in favour of Shia beliefs, *Muntahi-ul-Kalam*.

On the Sunnis' behalf, Maulvi Lutf Ullah wrote many books and Mulla Moin of Firangi Mahal criticised the Shia practice of Muta marriage in *Risal-e-Moinia*.

Poets were not untouched by this religious duel. A Shia poet, Mian Mushir, penned many satirical poems. He, along with his publisher, was prosecuted for his work *Kantap*.

In 1853, a converted Shia prince, Mirza Shikoh, originally from Delhi but settled in Lucknow, wrote *Ilm-I-Haideri dar Aqaide Salatin-I-Taimuri*, opining that all Mughal rulers were Shias by conviction. At this juncture, the great poet Mirza Ghalib — who was a Shia, but was financially supported by the Sunni emperors of Delhi and was known to speak on their behalf — joined the debate and wrote a masnawi refuting Shikoh's claim, which was in turn countered by Shikoh.

Poets who Ruled Awadh

Contrary to the assertions of British historians, quite a few Nawabs of Awadh were culturally evolved rulers and a good number of them were acknowledged poets.

The fourth Nawab, Asif-ud-daulah, who also built the magnificent Asifi Imambara, was an established poet. He was the pupil of the popular poet, Meer Soz. A sample of his poetic ability is this couplet from one of his many ghazals:

> *Where we see his sword aloft,*

> *There we found our heads roll down*

The fifth Nawab, Wazir Ali, whose rule was short-lived, was also a good poet; his poetry found resonance in all sections of contemporary society. He wrote verses that were full of pathos.

It is believed that the sixth Nawab, Saadat Ali Khan, who gifted almost half of Awadh to the East India Company in return for the favour of being crowned the Nawab of Awadh, also composed verses. However, his work is not easily available.

The seventh Nawab, Ghazi-ud-din Haidar, who became the first king of Awadh on 14 August 1814 by paying one-and-a-half crore rupees to the British, wrote marsiya as well as manqabat, two different styles of poetry. However, the Ustaads — the cognoscenti — did not rate his poetry as very good.

The much-ridiculed eighth Nawab, Nasir-ud-din Haidar, who ruled between 1827 and 1837 and was poisoned by Dhaniya Mehari on 8 July 1837, was good at writing qasida (panegyric) and ghazals. The following lines provide a sample of his poetry:

> *Ever since have my eyes beheld you,*

Wherever I see, I see, you alone

The eleventh and last Nawab, Wajid Ali Shah, was a prolific poet. His pen name was Akhtar, and he wrote almost all styles of poetry like hajo (satirical), marsiya (elegy, dirge), ghazal (amatory song or poem), masnawi (verse), salam (a form of religious poetry) and nauha (mourning poetry). The poetry of Wajid Ali Shah is considered to be the best among all the Nawabs.

The Art of Calligraphy

Calligraphy, in Awadh, was viewed as a form of art, and people who were experts in it, were respected in society on par with musicians, painters or any other artist.

One of the reasons why calligraphy became so popular was that it became a trend among the affluent and the cultured to decorate their houses with quotes written in beautiful handwriting, for which they did not mind spending a lot of money. This kind of calligraphy was called Nastaliq. Mir Ali Tabrezi, from Deylam, standardised the rules for Nastaliq. After Mir Ali Tabrezi, another artist, Mir Amad al Hasani, reached greater heights in this field and is considered by many as one of the most talented calligraphists ever.

The other prominent calligraphist from Deylam was Tabrezi's nephew, Agha Abdur Rashid, who had accompanied Nadir Shah when he invaded India. Rashid settled in Lahore where he began teaching calligraphy. Two of his brightest students, Qazi Nemat Ullah and Hafiz Nur Ullah, Persians, migrated to Lucknow after learning this art from him. In Awadh, they were promptly engaged by the royal family. Qazi Nemat was assigned the job of teaching techniques of good handwriting to royal princes, while Hafiz Nur was accommodated in the court. Their arrival began a new era. They taught a large number of people the intricacies of this art.

How well they were received in Lucknow, can be gauged by the market trend in those days, whereby even their routine work was sold at the rate of one rupee per letter. This made them not just comfortable, but rich members of society.

The sixth ruler Nawab, Saadat Ali Khan, was a great admirer of the Persian poet, Shaikh Sadi, a native of Shiraz. The Nawab liked Shaikh Sadi's work *Gulistan* so much that he always kept a copy

Calligraphy

Calligraphist Hafiz Nur Ullah

around. Once, he asked Hafiz Nur to copy out the manuscript in his handwriting. Hafiz asked the Nawab for eighty reams of paper, and one hundred penknives to sharpen thousands of bamboo quills. A shocked Saadat Ali asked him to explain why he required all this for one manuscript only. Hafiz's reply was businesslike: 'Sir, I always use this much.' Once he had all the required materials, he started writing, but it was so time-consuming, he could only finish seven chapters in his lifetime; he died while working on the eighth. Later, his son, Hafiz Ibrahim, who was given a black khilat by Saadat Ali to mourn his father's death, completed the manuscript.

Hafiz Nur Ullah had a Hindu pupil, Munshi Sarab Singh, who was either a Kashmiri Pandit or Kayastha. His work was so influenced by his mentor, it was difficult for even experts to distinguish between the two. Another of Hafiz Ibrahim's Hindu pupils, Munshi Mansa Ram, who was a Kashmiri Pandit, made a name for himself in Lucknow.

Begums

Procurement of the Fairies

~

Almost all the rulers of Awadh shared a common passion for talented and beautiful women. Always ready to increase the number of women in their harem, they used all the tricks in the bag.

In 1827, when Nasir-ud-din Haider became the king of Awadh, he appointed two officials — Lala Ram Prasad and Maharaja Mewa Ram — whose job it was to acquire beautiful women from various places and have them join the Nawab's harem. This group of women was known as Aish (pleasure) Mahal. The noted courtesan of the time, Karam Bux, was an Aish Mahal. Nasir-ud-din's debauchery was insatiable; even his famous prime minister, Roshan-ud-daula, provided him a courtesan named Hussaini, alias Mahbuban, from his own harem to ingratiate himself with the Nawab.

Nawab Amjad Ali Shah, the founder of Lucknow's famous market, Hazratganj, was a devout Muslim, but not devoid of a weakness for women. He had created a department of entertainers, known as Mohkama-e-Arbab-e-Nishat, and did not mind manipulating the men of his court to cater to his requirements. Rajab Ali Beg Suroor, a writer and literary person who was employed in the court for some time, was openly hostile to him, and spoke of him as, 'He who sends his youthful daughter inside', or 'If the sister is attending on the king, then the brother is his counsellor'.

In those days, good-looking girls were much in demand to replenish the Nawabs' harems. Pimps and procurers roamed across the countryside on the lookout for suitable catches. Upon spotting a pretty face in a poor family, they either purchased or enticed the girl away. Kidnapping was also common: Umrao Jaan Ada, the famous courtesan and protagonist of the eponymous book by Mirza Hadi Ruswa, was abducted and later sold to a procurer.

An Inmate of Parikhana

The last of the Nawabs, Wajid Ali Shah, whose rule started in 1847, had many channels by which women were collected for his harem; he was more organised than the other Nawabs in this regard. Besides Mir Mohammad Mehdi, from his department of entertainers, his chief procurers were the daroga (chief supervisor) of the harem, Najmunnisa Begum, and two sisters, Amman and Imaman.

This team recruited bewitching and beautiful women from different regions (though chiefly from amongst the courtesans of Lucknow) for the Nawab's harem, known as Pari Khana (House of Fairies), and the inmates were called paries (fairies). They were paid Rs 500 to Rs 1,500, depending on their talent and looks. There were about 150 women in the Pari Khana and Nawab Wajid Ali had Muta (temporary) marriage with most of them.

Wajid Ali Shah himself wrote in his memoirs about the other methods that were used to procure girls: 'The employee of the department of entertainers, whose name was Mahdi and who was posted as such in the reign of Jannat Makan [Amjad Ali Shah], persuaded a courtesan, Mahboob Jan, who was known far and wide for playing the sarod and dancing, to [come to] me under a pretext...he thought it was in his interest and conducive to his promotion to bring someone forcibly or under a false plea to me...'

Once the begums, the legitimate wives of Wajid Ali Shah, realised that they could no longer hold the Nawab's interest, they suggested, and even delivered, hand-picked, beautiful girls to him. Begum Nawab Nishat Mahal seconded the entry of Shah Bux, Wazir Pari and Altaf Bux into Wajid Ali Shah's Pari Khana. Wajid Ali Shah had this to say about this episode: 'As she [Nawab Khas Mahal] was wise and intelligent, she understood it well that her purpose would not be served unless she obeyed me and carried out my orders. Therefore she started sending women to serve me clandestinely.'

An Inmate of Parikhana

An Inmate of Parikhana

Although their harems were full, the Nawabs' appetite was so insatiable, they often preyed even on women who visited the palace to perform menial jobs. For example, Wajid Ali's father, Nawab Amjad Ali Shah, was so carried away by the charms of a woman who used to visit the palace to sell vegetables, he made her his wife.

Wajid Ali was one step ahead. Floored by the beauty of a young female water-carrier who was doing her job in the harem, he married her and gave her the title of 'Nawab Abrash Begum'. In the same fashion, the charms of a young scavenger girl proved too irresistible to him, and was given the title of 'Nawab Musaffa Begum'.

The Nawab's Daughter

While leaving his native place Nishapur in the Khurasan province of Iran, Saadat Khan promised his widowed sister that, if fortune favoured him in India, he would take care of her son. He kept his word. After establishing the Awadh dynasty in the year 1722, he appointed his sister's son, Safdar Jung, as the next in command and married one of his five daughters, Sadr-i-Jahan Begum, to him. Safdar Jung was ardently devoted to his wife; he had no mistress, courtesan or concubine.

Sadr-i-Jahan Begum was a very intelligent and strong-willed woman. Because of her exposure, she was deft in handling political situations. Apart from this, time and again she proved her exceptional ability to convince and motivate people around her. One example of this is her role after her husband Nawab Safdar Jung lost the battle of Ram Chatauni to the Pathans in 1750. The Turks of the Mughal Emperor tried to capitalise on this situation by conspiring to usurp Nawab Safdar Jung's estate and deprive him of his Vazarat. But they failed in their mission because of Sadr-i-Jahan Begum. She organised an army of 10,000 troops and garnered the support of her son, Shuja-ud-daulah and other important persons, to defend Safdar Jung.

The astute begum once bailed out her womaniser son from a difficult situation. Nawab Shuja-ud-daulah, floored by the beauty of an eighteen-year-old Khatri girl, abducted her for a night. This act turned quite a few people, especially the Khatris, against him. Some Mughal nobles decided to intervene and tried to topple Shuja-ud-daulah. Sadr-i-Jahan Begum prudently called the nobles and addressed them so convincingly that, according to author Sheik Tassaduq Hussain, her orations had the desired effect.

In the year 1764, she advised her son to support the ruler

of Bengal, Mir Qasim, in fighting the British. And, while Nawab Shuja-ud-daulah was preparing to fight in the battle of Buxar, Sadr-i-Jahan Begum asked him to bring back twelve British prisoners from the battlefield who would carry her palanquin.

Sadr-i-Jahan Begum also constructed an Imambara and a mosque behind Moti Bagh at Faizabad.

Unfortunately, Sadr-i-Jahan Begum was later harassed and tortured by her own grandson, Nawab Asif-ud-daulah, who, according to author K.S. Santha, robbed her of her property. The British did not help her because they suspected that she was siding with Chet Singh, Raja of Banaras, against them.

She died a disappointed person in 1796.

The Chequered Life of Bahu Begum

There are very few people whose life is as chequered as that of Ummatul Zohra, the chief wife of Nawab Shuja-ud-daulah. Ummatul Zohra was popularly known as 'Bahu Begum' in the palace household, a phrase that is a beautiful blend of Hindi and Turkish: 'Bahu' in Hindi means 'daughter-in-law' and 'begum' is a Turkish word for 'wife'.

She was the daughter of an Iranian noble, Mohammed Khan Motum-ud-daulah, in the Mughal court of Delhi, and her brother, Mohammad Ishaq Khan Najm-ud-daulah, was also an important noble in Emperor Mohammad Shah's court. The family's status and the relations they enjoyed with royalty are evidenced by the fact that her marriage was negotiated and performed by the emperor himself. According to K.S. Santha, author of *Begums of Awadh*, her marriage was a lavish, expensive one, costing Rs 46 lakhs — and this in 1745 A.D.

Ummatul Zohra was the richest of all the begums of Awadh. She owned a large jagir — which included places like Gonda, Jais, Khara, Allta, Rukka, Parsiddipur, Mohanganj, Salon and Simrauta — as well as zilas like Nawab Ganj, Garahiya Khas, Begum Bari, Mirganj and Sindh. Bahu Begum was entitled to collect taxes from the meat market and branding of cattle in her territory. Apart from this, she owned an extraordinary collection of jewellery, several houses and gardens.

This wealthy begum managed her jagir with the help of about 10,000 regular and irregular soldiers, and by posting in her area collectors, sub-collectors, tahsildars, police officials, attendants, zamindars and letter writers, who were all controlled by her loyal eunuchs. Her force of two thousand horsemen was under the command of one Ahmad Ali, and a fleet of twenty-five boats was at her disposal to travel on the river.

It is said she was a firm believer in destiny: apart from a physician, there was also one astrologer attendant in her court. According to writer Faiz Bux, nearly a lakh people depended on her directly or indirectly. Faiz Bux further writes: 'No woman in all thirty-two subahs in India can be held up as her rival in either the grandeur of her surroundings or the respect she could command.'

Bahu Begum was very loyal to her husband, Shuja-ud-daulah. After the defeat of Buxar, she went to great lengths to help him out financially; she even gave him her nose ring. He too valued her advice in matters of the state. For these reasons, many nobles sought her support. Bahu Begum lived in a large palace and to meet her one had to cross three gates guarded by eunuchs and female soldiers. The kind of authority, respect and popularity she enjoyed was unparalleled in the Awadh dynasty.

Bahu Begum

Her power and popularity made her appear almost like a de facto ruler of Faizabad; the British and other rulers of Awadh both feared and respected her. It is said that her son Asif-ud-daulah shifted his capital from Faizabad to Lucknow to escape from her influence in the court and lead a life of his own.

Bahu Begum unfortunately had an extremely unlucky streak too: Nawab Shuja-ud-daulah was a womaniser and had a number of wives, concubines and mistresses. Out of respect for her, he visited their palaces only clandestinely, but Bahu Begum knew what he was doing, and sarcastically referred to these buildings as 'Chor Mahal' (thieves' palaces).

The famous work *Sawanihat-i-Salatin-i-Awadh* mentions an incident when Bahu Begum once wanted to see her husband's children from his other wives. But when a large number of children were introduced to her, she could not control herself and began weeping bitterly.

She also had to face much abuse at the hands of her only son, Asif-ud-daulah, her protégé Haider Beg Khan, and a former employee, Murtaza Khan.

Nawab Asif-ud-daulah, with the help of the British, humiliated and tortured her in order to extort money from her. Instrumental in this was a former employee at her late husband's court, Murtaza Khan, who had been thrown out for misconduct by Shuja-ud-daulah. Bahu Begum was forced to give Asif-ud-daula Rs 31 lakhs, 70 elephants, 860 bullock carts and precious articles and gems. According to author K.S. Santha, in order to make her pay more, Murtaza Khan undervalued all the items and demanded Rs 11 lakhs over what she had given.

The unlucky begum also faced betrayal from a minister, Haider Beg Khan. The minister had once been in trouble for embezzling a large sum of money, and was saved from severe punishment only because of the begum's intervention. Haider Beg Khan was not grateful, however. When Nawab Asif-ud-daulah had to give one crore rupees to the British, Haider Beg manipulated the British and Asif-ud-daulah to confiscate Bahu Begum's jagirs on alleged charges of supporting a rebellion. Thanks to these devious machinations, Asif-ud-daulah gained Rs 50 lakhs in cash and another Rs 50 lakhs in kind.

After Asif-ud-daulah's death in 1797, Nawab Wazir Ali became the ruler with Bahu Begum's consent. The begum regained her earlier influence and again became a very important figure. This glory, however, was short-lived: differences between her and the Nawab crept up, and when the British decided to dethrone him, she supported the move. Her stepson, Nawab Saadat Ali Khan, was then crowned the ruler of Awadh.

Unfortunately this move boomeranged on her, for Saadat Ali Khan coveted her property. To save her assets, she put them in the care of the British. The British in turn tried to create confusion between her and Saadat Ali's successor, Nawab Ghazi-ud-din Haider, for fear that she might take her assets back and place them with Ghazi-ud-din.

This most powerful but unfortunate begum of Awadh, who suffered betrayal by her near and dear ones, died in 1815.

Nawab Asif-ud-daulah

A Fine for not spending the Night

The Battle of Buxar in 1764 proved the turning point in the history of Awadh. Nawab Shuja-ud-daulah, the third ruler of Awadh, acting on the advice of his mother, Sadr-i-Jahan, supported the Nawab of Bengal. He fought against the British but lost the battle and was forced to compromise on very humiliating terms, which included a payment to the British.

After the war, the Nawab did not have the money required to regain his royal status from the British. He approached his relatives and highly placed courtiers but not much help was forthcoming from them. It was at this time that his chief wife, Bahu Begum, proved herself. She gave to her husband all the property, jewellery and cash she had. It is on record, that she even gave him her precious pearl-studded nose ring. According to *Sier-ul-Mutakhirin,* when people close to her advised her against parting with everything she had, she replied that everything she possessed would lose its value, if her husband ceased to live.

Although Shuja-ud-daulah could be called debauched — his harem comprised more than seven hundred inmates — he never forgot his chief spouse's loyalty at the time of his crisis. He loved and respected her so much that, despite his relentless philandering, he made it a point to eat both meals of the day with Bahu Begum and spend the night at her palace. Whenever Shuja-ud-daulah, due to his weakness for other women, failed to spend the night with her, he paid Bahu Begum Rs 5,000 for that night!

Blind Love

An example of how a mother's love for her spoiled son can ruin her own life, is the relationship between the fourth ruler, Nawab Asif-ud-daulah and his mother, Bahu Begum.

Nawab Shuja-ud-daulah was disappointed by his son, Asif-ud-daulah, and was considering declaring his other son, Saadat Ali Khan, who at that time was known as Mirza Mangli, as his successor. But Bahu Begum, Asif-ud-daulah's mother, blinded by maternal love, forced her husband to reconsider his decision in favour of her son. She even ignored her mother-in-law, Sadr-i-Jahan, who adviced against making Asif-ud-daulah heir to the throne. But soon after her husband's death, she realised her mistake.

Asif-ud-daulah, within ten days of his father's demise, went to Mehdi Ghat on a pleasure trip, and sent his minister Murtaza Khan to his mother with a demand for money to meet his expenses. When Bahu Begum's brother, Salar Jung, who had also been sent with the minister, approached her, she asked him, 'Has Asif-ud-daulah no time to shed a tear for his father?' After this, according to the *Memoirs of Delhi and Faizabad*, the loving mother oscillated for about two to three days before paying her son Rs 6 lakh.

Her son, in a short span of time, spent all the money, and again approached his mother through her other brother, Mirza Ali Khan, for more money. Bahu Begum was extremely unhappy, but reluctantly gave another Rs 4 lakh. However, for her son even this amount was not sufficient, so he himself came to Faizabad and forced his mother to procure a loan of Rs 4 lakh against the guarantee of certain areas of her jagir.

Having now realised Asif-ud-daulah's profligate ways, Bahu Begum was completely disillusioned with him.

Badsha Begum's Last Days

After Nasir-ud-din Haider's death and the ensuing tussle over the throne, Badsha Begum and her protégé Munna Jan were sent by the British to Chunar Fort as prisoners. Badsha Begum described her arrest in a complaint to the Governor-General. According to the book *Tarikh-i-Badsha Begum*, she said that she was dragged away from the palace along with the young prince, Munna Jan. They were taken on foot to the Residency where they were locked up like wild beasts and kept in a state of near starvation.

In the first two days they were imprisoned in two different rooms of the Zard Kothi. But Munna Jan cried so much that the Resident, moved by his plight, instructed his staff to keep them in one room. According to Abdu Ahad, author of *Tarikh-i-Badsha Begum,* the English soldiers guarding them did not allow anyone to meet them, except the person who served them food. The first queen of Awadh was so shocked to find herself in confinement, that for two days she did not eat anything: only on the third day did she eat a little bit along with Munna Jan. But during these three days she performed all her religious rituals fully and was always found reading the holy Quran.

The local population of Lucknow by and large was in her favour, and the Resident was afraid that there could be a problem of law and order in the city. King Mohammad Ali Shah, newly appointed by the British, was also scared of Badsha Begum's presence in the capital and he requested the Resident to keep her in confinement out of Awadh at his expense. Thus it was decided to send her to Chunar. From Lucknow she was first sent to Kanpur with orders from the Resident to Commander Stevenson in Kanpur that the begum should be treated well, but at the same time security should not be in the least relaxed. He specially recommended keeping an eye on her servants so that the begum could not escape posing as a

King Mohammad Ali Shah

servant. After the begum's departure, the Resident sent eighteen cartloads of goods and eighteen slave girls for the comfort of the royal prisoners.

According to Mrs Fanny Parks' book *Wanderings of a Pilgrim*, the begum, along with Munna Jan, reached Allahabad on 17 October 1837 and stayed there a day or two. During their stay at Allahabad, their tent was surrounded by guards. From there they were forced to march and finally, when Munna Jan, and Badsha Begum reached Chunar, they were imprisoned in the fort with the same strict restrictions as applied at Kanpur. But with each passing day some liberty was given, till at last the rules were as relaxed as royal prisoners deserved. The ruling king Mohammad Ali Shah also allocated, from 1 December 1838, an amount of Rs 1,800 per month for her, Rs 600 for Munna Jan, and Rs 100 for their in-charge, Captain Stewart.

Despite all adversities, Badsha Begum did not give up the claim for the throne. She and her outside supporters conspired to appeal to the British authority in England for justice. But this was detected at an early stage, and Mohammad Ali Shah recommended to the British that, by this act of hers, she had lost her right to the monthly income allocated to her. In the new situation she also ran the risk of being separated from her grandson and deported to a distant place.

At this juncture, the Governor-General intervened and she was persuaded by all concerned parties to give a written undertaking that she had no claims to the throne of Awadh. By this time, due to the unprecedented humiliation and her advanced age, Badsha Begum had become very weak. She gave in to the demands and gave the desired undertaking in exchange for a stipend of Rs 3,700. The same kind of undertaking was given by Munna Jan also, who died on 11 January 1846, probably due to a ruptured blood vessel in the head. This last blow added to her misery and within a few months Badsha Begum died. Both of them were buried in adjoining graves at Chunar.

A Tawaif becomes a Queen

The famous writer Fanny Parks, in her work *Wanderings of a Pilgrim*, describes the beauty of Nawab Nasir-ud-din Haidar's wife Taj Mahal in the following words: 'I could think of nothing but Lalla Rookh in her bridal attire. I never saw anyone so lovely, either black or white. Her features were perfect and such eyes and eyelashes, I never beheld before.....She was so graceful and swanlike. This beautiful creature is the envy of all other wives.'

The charming Begum Taj Mahal's real name was Hussainee and she was the daughter of the famous tawaif Bhajhu, a resident of Haznpur Bandhwa. The beautiful Hussainee had mastered the art of dance and music at an early stage of her life and started giving performances at marriages. According to *Begamat-i-Awadh*, Nawab Nasir-ud-din saw her performing in one of these functions and immediately decided to marry her. He gave her the title of 'Khurshid Mahal' but it became redundant because one day, according to *Sawanihat-i-Salatin-i-Awadh*, the Nawab placed his crown on Hussainee's head and called her 'Taj Mahal'. And it was this name that became more popular.

The Nawab tried to hide the murkier side of her lineage. He fabricated a story that a man, Mirza Hussain Beg, was her father. This 'father' was appointed the in-charge of Nawabganj, which was given to her. Apart from this, the Nawab also included her name in an agreement with the British to provide her a monthly income of Rs 6,000.

Unfortunately for Taj Mahal, these days did not last long, for soon the Nawab shifted his love and attention to another wife, Badsha Mahal. This was too much for Taj Mahal to bear, so in frustration she started drinking. This habit indirectly did some good to her, because though she was no longer as important to him as earlier, the Nawab started drinking with her.

A Begum of Awadh

After the death of the Nawab in 1837, Taj Mahal went through a difficult time. Twice she was made to vacate her palace. First, she was asked by the new Nawab, Mohammad Ali Shah, to leave the royal dwelling and move to a house where she lived till 1844. The second time, she was ordered to shift from her palace by his son and the tenth ruler, Amjad Ali Shah. He gave her the option of three houses, but she refused to oblige him. At last the British Resident, Pollock, had to interfere on behalf of the ruler, who on the threat of suspending her pension from the treasury, had the palace vacated.

In her later years, Taj Mahal suffered at both British and the Indian hands. At the time of the first freedom struggle in 1857, Begum Hazrat Mahal levied a tribute of one lakh rupees on her. She also had to pay Rs 39,000 to the British through the city magistrate, Major Carnagie. This act of hers offended the freedom fighters, who plundered her palace.

Although she was loyal to the British during the struggle, to her disappointment, when the freedom struggle was over and the British regained power, they imposed on her a levy of Rs 12,000. A dejected Taj Mahal pleaded with the British and gave the example of other begums like Surfraz Mahal, Mumtaz Mahal and Begum Malika Jahan who were exempted from war tax. After much persuasion the Rs 12,000 was given back to her.

A disillusioned Taj Mahal later moved to Mecca, where she married Mir Kalb-e-Hussain. She breathed her last in Iraq in 1881.

113

Iraq in the Heart of Lucknow

The seventh Nawab of Awadh, Ghazi-ud-din Haidar, who managed to declare himself as the first king of Awadh on October 1819 by obliging the British with money, was a short-tempered man. However, his softer side was revealed when it came to his dealings with the poor.

Najaf, in Iraq, is considered holy for Shias: a mausoleum here is presumed to be the burial place of Hazrat Ali, the son-in-law of Prophet Mohammad. King Ghazi-ud-din Haidar realised that economically-backward Shias could not meet the expenses of the journey to this far-off city. So, he constructed a replica of the tomb in Lucknow, which is now known as Shah Najaf Imambara.

Ghazi-ud-din did not trust his heirs with its maintenance, so he deposited enough money with the British, so that the interest on the principal would pay for the upkeep of the Imambara. It is because of this farsighted arrangement that, even today, the lamps are lit on the tomb and the place is beautifully illuminated during Muharram.

Finally, according to his wishes, when Ghazi-ud-din died on 18 October 1827, he was buried in this Imambara.

Located on the banks of the river Gomati, this magnificent edifice does not conform with that of a standard Imambara. For instance, its main entrance on the northern side faces the river, while the southern entrance, facing the road, is closed. Also, the outermost gateway is not in alignment with the main enclosure.

One interesting fact about the Imambara is that three of Ghazi-ud-din's begums, hailing from three different religions — Hinduism, Islam and Christianity — are buried here along with him.

The first to be interred at this grand mausoleum was Begum Ghairatunnisa Mubarak Mahal.

Begum Ghairatunnisa Mubarak Mahal was born a Christian; christened Sidney Hay, she was the daughter of a Colonel Aish, and a native woman, Champa. A talented woman, she had penned the popular book *Historic Lucknow*. Ghazi-ud-din was swept off his feet by her immense talent and beauty when he chanced upon her in Kanpur, where he had gone to receive the Governor-General, Lord Warren Hastings. So enamoured was Ghazi-ud-din of her that, through Wazir Agha Mir's subtle and deft manoeuvring, he had her brought to Lucknow. She converted to Islam (Shia) before he married her in 1815. She was just sixteen then, while Ghazi-ud-din was well over thirty-seven.

Ghazi-ud-din was very much in love with Begum Ghairatunnisa Mubarak Mahal. He named a garden Villayati Bagh after her ('villayati' in Urdu means foreigner). This 'villayati' begum, who never observed purdah, died on 30 January 1840, and was buried at the Shah Najaf Imambara beside the king.

Begum Sarfaraz Mahal, a dusky, extremely attractive girl, was originally from Malihabad. Born Husaini Khanam into a Sunni family, she converted to the Shia faith when she married Ghazi-ud-din. She was given a wasiqa of Rs 1,000 per month for her personal use, and Rs 639 a month to maintain domestic help. As she was very religious, she used to send one-third of this amount to Karbala Sharif. As a widow, she lived in Machchi Bhawan. The British had used the building to house ammunition during the first war of independence in 1857. When they failed to shift the ammunition to the Residency, they blew up and razed the building to the ground. After the building was razed down, Begum Sarfaraz Mahal moved to a large house in Mahmood Nagar. She died at seventy, on 28 October 1878, and was buried at Shah Najaf Imambara.

The last of the three begums to be laid to rest along with Ghazi-ud-din, was a Hindu by birth. Begum Mumtaz Mahal's father, Urai

Lal, converted to Islam. Since her name and that of King Nasir-ud-din's mother was the same, she was called Mumtaz Mahalshani. She built a mosque, which still exists in Mohalla Chandi Khana.

After the death of Ghazi-ud-din, she dressed only in white, and lived behind the Imambara where her husband was buried. She died in 1896, and was buried at the same place, along with her husband and his Christian and Muslim begums.

Bribes for a Begum

Abuse of one's power or influence, is a phenomenon that has occurred across the ages all over the world. But influence whimsically wielded could overnight turn a protégé into a bete noir and vice versa. Nothing illustrates this better than the lifestyle of the wife of the eighth ruler of Awadh, Nawab Nasir-ud-din Haidar. Bismilla Khanam, alias Qudsia Mahal, as she was known, married the Nawab on 17 December 1831. As long as the prime minister of Awadh, Muntazm-ud-daulah Hakim Mehdi Ali Khan, kept her in good humour, he enjoyed his position and post. But once his economy drive, which he had launched to reduce state expenditure, affected her, and after he offended her maid, Atooji, she became the cause of his ouster.

Then, with the help of the Nawab's mother, Badsha Begum, she played a crucial role in the appointment of a new prime minister, Roshan-ud-daulah. The wily Roshan-ud-daulah had approached the begum by sending an application for the post through her maid Atooji. The begum's clique decided that Roshan-ud-daulah would be the most 'manageable' and submissive person to head the administration. As per their plan, the begum presented this application at an appropriate time to the Nawab along with her recommendation and personal insistence. The Nawab was so much under the influence of his wife that, after reading the contents of the letter, he did not say a single word but simply burnt the letter with a candle; the very next day Roshan-ud-daulah was made his deputy and honoured with a khilat, the robe of honour.

Prime Minister, Roshan-ud-daulah

Roshan-ud-daulah was well aware of the power of the clique through whose largesse he had obtained his new exalted position and status. At times he felt as if he were a puppet in their hands. He let the British Resident know about his helplessness and that the actual power was in the hands of Qudsia Begum and her coterie including, among others, Badsha Begum and Subhan Ali Khan.

Although Roshan-ud-daulah had mentioned quite a few names, in reality, the real power was in the hands of Qudsia Begum who had few qualms about misusing it to her advantage. She not only accumulated wealth, but was also ready to go to any extent to save her protégés and defend the wrongs done by them. As per the report 'Affairs of Oude', 1834, No. 88, Qadir Khan, Atooji's son, manipulated the arrest of a banker, Chowdhury of Rodouli, on fabricated charges. After bringing him to Lucknow like a prisoner, Qadir Khan forced him to pay Rs 30,000. No action was taken against Qadir Khan because of the begum's intervention. The Amil of Salon, Dhookul Singh — who, on the pretext of arresting two absconding zamindars, went to Amethi parganas with his three battalions and six guns and plundered the village — was also protected by the begum.

Another of her protégés, Hussain Beg, became so notorious for using her patronage to harass residents of Byswara, that the Resident was forced to intervene.

Once, the prime minister wanted to appoint his son as Naib, the Commander of the forces, but Qudsia Begum wanted to appoint one, Lalji, who had assured her that she would benefit monetarily if he were given the post. In the final show of strength, the begum sent a message to the prime minister through Atooji warning him that, if Lalji was not appointed, she would see to it that his services were terminated. It had the desired effect and Lalji was given the appointment in exchange for a bribe of Rs 60,000. Of this, Qudsia Begum retained Rs 40,000 and Rs 20,000 was given to prime minister Roshan-ud-daulah to appease him.

A Rags-to-Riches Story

Qudsia Mahal had fought hard to reach the position that she eventually did. Hers was very much a rags-to-riches story.

Before marrying Nawab Nasir-ud-din Haidar, Qudsia Mahal was an economically backward, married woman who constantly quarrelled with her husband, Mir Haidar or Mirza Bhujju Beg. She worked at the palace as a maid. One of her children had died, and the other was looked after by her parents.

She was first employed by the mother of the Nawab and later moved on to serve Taj Mahal, one of the Nawab's wives. It was when she began serving another wife of the Nawab, Malika-i-Zamani, that her destiny took a turn for the better. It was during this tenure that she met the ruling Nawab, Nasir-ud-din Haidar. W.H. Sleeman gives very interesting details of their meeting: he says the king was very pleased by her bold spirit and charm and decided to marry her.

As per the Nawab's wish, her husband was asked to divorce her and leave Lucknow, for which he was provided considerable allowance. So, according to this arrangement, her husband, after divorcing her, went away to Kanpur. The Nawab married Qudsia as per Shia rituals on 17 December 1831 and conferred on her the title of 'Mukhadara-i-Zaman Mehdi Uzma Bilquis Dauran Malika Afaq Qudsia Sultan Mariam Bano Begum'.

Nawab Nasir-ud-din was so besotted by Qudsia Begum, he gave her 15,000 gold mohars and a chest full of precious jewels. Apart from this, he deposited Rs 33 lakhs at the rate of four percent with the British Government, with the condition that its interest would be paid to Qudsia Begum and that the British would provide her protection. He later added Rs 18 lakhs to this sum.

The Nawab was so generous with her, that, from the time of her marriage till her death, a period of four years, he had gifted her about Rs 4 crore. Since she felt God was blessing her with His bounty, she in turn tried to be good to people around her. According to Sheikh Tassadq Hussain's *Begamat-i-Awadh*, Qudsia never touched her food until alms worth Rs 500 were distributed to the poor. This begum, after using her gold and silver jewellery for a year, distributed it among her staff.

There is one more case recorded in *Begamat-i-Awadh*, which demonstates her approach towards money. Once, when her money bags had been taken out to be counted, a maid stole a bag and hid it in the bathroom. When the crime was found out and reported to the begum, she refused to take back the money bag stating that it had become impure by being deposited in such a place. She ordered that it be given to back to maid. While some were of the opinion that these acts were whimsical, for local historians these were acts of generosity in disguise.

Once, a dyer, hearing about her helpful nature, went to her and asked for financial help to facilitate a marriage in his family. She inquired about the amount he required, and when he revealed that he wanted just a few hundreds of rupees, she refused and asked him not to approach her with a similar plea again. Surprised by her reaction, the dyer later discovered that she did not like anyone approaching her for such a small amount.

Qudsia Begum lived in style. She spent Rs 1,400 per day on her kitchen, which had famous chefs like Pir Ali, an expert in preparing samosas. This begum felt she had everything in life except a son from Nawab Nasir-ud-din Haider, whom she could have declared as successor to the throne. She was so desperate to have a son that, according to historian K.S. Santha, 'Not being sure of Nasir-ud-din Haidar, she called her former husband from Kanpur who met her secretly for six to seven days. The resulting pregnancy ended in a miscarriage on 20 September 1833. She tried once more, but this intrigue was discovered by the King.'

Nawab Nasir-ud-din Haidar

The Nawab had a heated argument with the begum on 21 August 1834, and in a fit of anger told her that it was he who had raised her from the gutters to the royal throne and he could send her back there as easily. This insult was too much to bear for Qudsia Begum, so she took out the poison that she always carried in the locket of her necklace, and consumed it. The shocked Nawab tried everything, but could not save her. Later on, the Nawab declared a forty-day mourning period at the court.

The Nawab's English Wife

One of the wives of the eighth Nawab, Nasir-ud-din, was Muqaddar Ali. Nawab had married her because of her beauty. In *Begmat-i-Awadh*, she is described as having a delicate and charming personality. The Nawab had given her a jagir consisting of Miyaganj, Unnao and Rasulabad that generated an annual income of Rs 6 lakh. According to *A Journey through the Kingdom of Oudh*, the Nawab had fixed a monthly pension of Rs 6,000 for her maintenance.

Apart from Persian and the local language, Begum Muqaddar Ali, who came from a Christian family, knew English very well. She took pains to teach English to her husband, Nasir-ud-din, for he was very fascinated by English culture and was eager to emulate it.

The begum had a very humble background. Her father, George Hopkins Walters, was a half pay officer and her mother was the daughter of an English businessman. After the untimely death of George Hopkins Walters, his wife moved with her children to Kanpur. The famous work *Wanderings of a Pilgrim*, records that the family experienced hard times and Mrs Walters barely managed by embroidering saddlecloths for horses of the rich.

In those days, a man, Buksh Ali, was engaged by the family as a coachman, although by profession he was a drummer. Buksh Ali gradually became closer to the family. And when Mrs Walters started worrying about the marriage of her grown-up daughters, he convinced her that she should shift her family to Lucknow as her daughters stood a better chance of marriage there.

After a lot of planning, Walters came to Lucknow and the daughters were introduced to Nawab Nasir-ud-din who opted for the younger daughter for marriage. Nawab married this Christian girl in the year 1827 as per Muslim rituals, and after this she was known as Begum Muqaddar Alia.

Although Nasir-ud-din had married a girl of lower status, according to *Begums of Awadh*, 'In order to maintain the prestige of [the] royal family, [the] King persuaded Buksh Ali to marry Mrs Walters and provided them with money and rank.' Nawab Nasir-ud-din's move was probably also motivated by the possibility that Mrs Walters and Buksh Ali had developed an intimate relationship that society would have disapproved of. The entire family converted to Islam and changed their names. The elder daughter became known as Sharf-un-nisa, and the son, Joseph Walters, changed his name to Amir Mirza.

A Virgin Queen's Apartment

Nasir-ud-din Haidar's chief wife, Ruqayya Sultan Begum, popularly known as Sultan Bahu, was the granddaughter of the Mughal Emperor of India, Shah Alam, and her grandmother, Qudsia Begum, hailed from the famous Safovia family of Iran. According to reports, Ruqayya Sultan was deeply hurt because her father, Prince Mirza Sulaiman Shikoh, of Delhi's royal family, practically forced to marry her to Nasir-ud-din.

In fact, her father, fed up with the palace intrigues of the Delhi court, migrated to Awadh during the reign of Nawab Asif-ud-daulah. Having settled down in Lucknow, he survived solely on the financial help and hospitality of the Nawabs of Awadh. Nawab Asif-ud-daulah and Saadat Ali Khan both treated him with respect as Awadh was part of the Mughal Empire. But the eighth ruler, Ghazi-ud-din Haidar, who had snapped ties with Delhi and declared himself an independent king, demanded equal status from Prince Sulaiman Shikoh, who after some initial reluctance agreed. Later on, Ghazi-ud-din proposed the marriage of his foster son, Nasir-ud-din, with Prince Shikoh's daughter. A go-between approached Nawazish Mahal, the chief wife of the Prince Shikoh and persuaded her to agree to the proposal. Prince Shikoh, being financially dependent on Ghazi-ud-din, could hardly refuse.

Author Fanny Parks writes: 'The beautiful Timonium Sultan Boa, the princess of Delhi was disgusted at her father being forced to give her in marriage to Nasir-ud-din Haidar and looked upon him as a man of a low caste, in comparison to herself.'

Apart from this grudge, the self-respecting Sultan Bahu could not reconcile with Nasir-ud-din's ever growing weakness for beautiful women. This charming woman, who was given the title of 'Malika-i-Dauran' at the time of her marriage, moved to

Husn Bagh soon after her wedding and lived on a small allowance given by Nasir-ud-din. Although there were enough reasons for her to drift away from her husband, according to W.H. Sleeman, ministers of the court, seeking to advance their own interests, also played an important role in creating misunderstandings between husband and wife.

All these valid or invalid reasons made her hate her husband, and as K.S. Santha writes, 'She so disliked his way of life that she did not permit him to enter her...residence.'

Parks also endorses this view about Sultan Bahu's unfulfilled married life and the fact that the Nawab was not allowed to enter the palace where the queen lived. She says, 'She never allowed him to enter her palace, a virgin queen's apartment.'

The Slave who Became Queen

History disappoints those who take pride in their family lineage. For it has enough examples to prove that, all over the world, dynasties were not necessarily founded by accepted or respected classes of that time.

Nawab Nasir-ud-din Haidar's life is one such interesting instance. His mother, Subhey Daulat, was a widowed washerwoman from Nanpara in Bahraich district. She was employed in the services of Badsha Begum, the chief begum of Nawab Ghazi-ud-din Haidar.

When working in the palace, the washerwoman, Subhey Daulat, became involved with the Nawab, and soon she became pregnant. Badsha Begum could not tolerate this, and after the birth of the baby, she got Subhey Daulat killed. She then adopted the child, Nasir-ud-din Haidar.

When it came to women, Nasir-ud-din Haidar proved to be a chip off the old block. When still a prince and already married, he could not resist the charm of a slave girl in the palace who was employed to feed his son Muna Jan. He married this slave girl in 1826 and gave her the title of 'Malka Zamani'.

Malka Zamani was the daughter of a poor Kori farmer of Varanasi and had been sold to a Muslim family. She had been married before to a man, Qaiwan Jah, who worked in a stable. She was rumoured to have had relationships with other men before marrying Nawab Nasir-ud-din Haidar; her affair with a Pathan was one of the more well known ones.

After the death of Nawab Ghazi-ud-din Haidar on 20 October 1827, Nasir-ud-din Haidar became the ruler of Awadh. At this juncture, Malka Zamani came to play such a central role in the life of the king, that Nasir-ud-din declared her son from her previous marriage as the heir apparent. She also managed to have her daughter from her previous marriage married to a grandson of the Mughal emperor Mohammad Ali Shah, and gained control of a jagir generating an income of Rs 6 lakh a year.

Fanny Parks, in her *Wanderings of a Pilgrim in Search of the Picturesque*, wrote, 'She has great power over her royal husband whose ears she boxes occasionally.'

Almost all the desires of this devout Shia slave girl, who became the Queen of Awadh, were fulfilled, all except her wish to have a child from her husband, Nawab Nasir-ud-din Haidar. According to Shiek Tassaduq Husain, it was for this reason that she visited the dargah of Hazrat Abbas at Lucknow on every Nauchandi Thursday.

Malka Zamani built a beautiful mosque and an impressive Imambara in Golaganj locality way back in 1837. After her death in 1843, she was buried in this very Imambara.

A Punishment for a Prince

The chief wife of the tenth ruler of Awadh, Amjad Ali Shah, was Malika-i-Kishwar, popularly known as Janab-i-Alia. The daughter of Nawab Hussain-ud-din Khan of Kalpi, Malika-i-Kishwar, was the mother of the last King of Awadh, Wajid Ali Shah.

This educated begum, who was fluent in Persian, saw to it that her personal staff at the palace too was educated, and for this purpose she appointed a teacher for them. At times she herself taught them. A sensitive woman, she refused to appoint any maid who had been brought to her palace by force.

The Governor-General, Lord Dalhousie, thought she was a very sensible, respectable lady who possessed a great deal of influence over her son and always used it very sagaciously. Impressed by her profile, W.H. Sleeman recommended her name for the Council of Regency, to help her son, Nawab Wajid Ali, and further suggested that she be consulted in the nomination of the members of this council.

She attached so much importance to her late husband's memories that when Wajid Ali wanted to replace Amjad Ali's coins with his name she said, 'Have a new coinage with your own image and subscription made. Deface not the image of your father. How shall that son obtain the favour of heaven, who mars his father's work?'

Malika-i-Kishwar never liked formal, gaudy royal dresses or the heavy ornaments that were meant to be worn with them. She did not like attending formal state processions either. These customs were tiresome for her, but, when she was required to go to England to plead her son's case with Queen Victoria after the kingdom was annexed by the British on 7 February 1856, she did not hesitate.

Malika-i-Kishwar failed in her mission, and on her way back to India, she died in Paris at the age of fifty-five. The Emperor and prime minister of France attended her funeral. While her funeral procession was moving to the burial place (a piece of land obtained from the area that was owned by the Ambassador of Rome), the prime minister of France made a touching gesture. Malika-i-Kishwar's young son, Hashmat Sikander, was walking with cortege, but a concerned prime minister made him sit in his chariot.

Michail Edwardes comments in the work *The Orchid House*, 'There is pathos about their reception and rejection which ended, oddly enough, in the cemetery of Pere Lachoise for the Queen mother.'

Like any other mother, Malika-i-Kishwar too loved her sons, but she did not let her affection spoil them. According to *Begums of Awadh*, 'She exercised a strict supervision during their childhood and continued to censor their undesirable acts when they grew up.'

There is an interesting incident described by K.S. Santha. Once, in the palace, mohars were kept out so they could be counted. Her second son, Mirza Sikandar Hashmat, stole a few. When the begum came to know about it, she was so angry that she got the prince's hands and feet tied like a criminal and placed him before the king for judgement and punishment. But contrary to her expectations, the king was not happy with this kind of treatment to his son, and instead of punishing him he lovingly fondled him. Although Sikandar Hashmat was her favourite son, she did not like the king's reaction to the whole episode, and as a punishment she did not let the boy move about for three days.

A Greengrocer's Daughter becomes Queen

~

Born in 1798, Surayya Shah sat on the throne of Awadh on 17 May 1842 as Amjad Ali Shah. He was married to an extremely beautiful young lady, popularly referred to as 'Janab-i-Alia'. She was his chief wife, and her family lineage was linked to the reputed family of Delhi's Khan-i-Khanan. Amjad Ali was very fond of her, but all her qualities could not stop him for falling in love with other women.

Janab-i-Alia, like any normal wife, was very jealous of other women who flirted with her husband. Once, when she discovered that her husband was carrying on an affair with one of her maidservants, she got the woman's face burnt. But even these inhumane protests failed to deter Amjad Ali Shah from indulging his weakness for charming women.

This most religious ruler of the Awadh dynasty, who strictly adhered to the principles of his religion when it came to governing his kingdom, followed the dictates of his heart when it came to romance. Considerations of caste, class, or age, did not interfere in his pursuits: a trend that continued till the end. Just one year before his death, at the age of forty-eight, he fell in love with a sixteen-year-old girl. She was the daughter of a greengrocer and had come to the royal palace to sell vegetables. The moment the Nawab saw her, he lost control over himself and believed that he could not live without her. Even the glaring age gap did not deter him and he finally married her. After marriage he conferred on her the title of 'Sultan Mahal'.

His love for Sultan Mahal was apparently quite deep, because in November 1846, when he invested money in Government notes for the future financial security of his wives, he made a provision for her also. According to *A Journey through the Kingdom of Oudh*,

Amjad Ali made a provision of rupees one lakh for Sultan Mahal. Unfortunately, Sultan Mahal was unable to enjoy her fortune.

The amount had been transferred to the British Resident's treasury in the form of five notes of Rs 20,000 denomination each. On 28 August, Sultan Mahal informed the Resident, in writing, that she had authorised her agent Saiyyad Muhammad to collect the money on her behalf. Unfortunately, she died the very next day. Immediately, the last ruler of Awadh, Wajid Ali Shah, staked his claim to this money, as heir of his father, Amjad Ali. At the same time, Sultan Mahal's mother and brother too, as *her* heirs, asserted their claim on the money. The British Resident decided the case in favour of her mother and brother. Wajid Ali Shah was not satisfied with this decision, so the case was sent to the Governor-General: but he too endorsed the Resident's decision.

How Royal Harems were Managed

All the Nawabs of Awadh — excluding the second Nawab, Safdar Jung — had a weakness for beautiful women. It was therefore to be expected that the Nawabs' harems teemed with several hundreds of charming women. And to manage such a large establishment, employees with special skills were recruited.

It is interesting to note that, even for the most ordinary kind of work, a specialised worker was deputed. Although the size of the service retinue varied according to the number and demands of the inmates, a few types of female help were common to all harems. They were known by different names. For example, mashshata were the women employed to help dress the royal women; and a dastango's job was to entertain the women by narrating interesting stories.

According to the writer Agha Mehdi, the woman entrusted with the education and etiquette of the young girls was called atu. The female employees who handled the paperwork and correspondence, were known as chitthinavis, while those who carried message from the entrance of the harem to the inside, were addressed as mahaldar.

Meer Hasan Ali explains that often the begums were reluctant to breastfeed their babies, fearing that it would spoil their figure, so they employed women called annas to do the same. Usually a young girl was engaged to clean the baby and keep it company. These girls were known as chhuchu. The women who taught toddlers to speak were called dadaju, and the women who brought up the child, were known as dada. The main job of the khelai was to keep the baby in good humour. Women selected to keep the daughters of begums company were referred to as sukhni; paid companions to royal ladies were called khawses. Female bearers were engaged to carry the palanquins of Nawabs and their ladies, and they were known as kaharis.

Aseels served in the kitchen, while mehris did different routine jobs, as per the instructions of queens. Mughlanis were given the task of stitching, while the tosha khana wali was the store and godown-keeper. Pesh khidmat conveyed the instructions of royal inmates to people.

Women with a religious bent of mind were hired to recite marsiya, soz, hadis and nauha. These were known as marsiya khwan, soz khwan, hadis khwan and nauha khwan, respectively.

Apart from this, an elderly lady, who as a young woman had worked as a chhuchu, was named bubu and dai, and was the personal servant of the bride, with whom she had entered the harem.

At the top of the hierarchy was the kaniz or bandi, who took general instructions from the queens. Writer Fida Ali Khanjar mentions that there was a chief mughlani to control the harem from inside, and khwaja sera, eunuchs, to manage it from outside.

Prostitute Arrested for Opposing Marriage

Wajid Ali Shah, whose opulent lifestyle was legendary in the subcontinent (his pulao was cooked with one gold coin), was surprisingly a teetotaller. In fact, he never consumed any intoxicating substance in his life.

His real weakness was women. He had only two wives, Nawab Khas Mahal and Akhtar Mahal, by Mankuha Nikahi, a type of permanent marriage, but several Muta'ai wives (married, as per the Muta marriage rituals of Shias, for a certain period).

Just as Wajid Ali Shah's famous sense of justice was above communal or class feelings, so was his love for female beauty. While he was still a prince and married to Nawab Khas Mahal, the beauty of a girl called Waziran floored him. This eighteen-year-old disarmingly beautiful girl lived on present-day Victoria Street.

Waziran came in touch with Wajid Ali through his younger brother, Mirza Sikandar Hashmat Bahadur. She was an excellent singer and dancer besides being exceptionally beautiful. Waziran was the daughter of a prostitute, Bi Jan, who for her own reasons, did not approve of her daughter consorting with the Nawab. She stridently resisted the prince's staff who had come to take her daughter to his privy chamber.

This unexpected turn of events made Wajid Ali long for Waziran even more. In a rage, he decided to shoot himself with a pistol. Fortunately, things soon took a turn to his satisfaction.

Wajid Ali, the heir apparent, and Waziran continued to meet clandestinely for about a month. At times they rendezvoused at his acquaintance Azim-ud-daulah's house at Golaganj. It was at one of these meetings that Wajid Ali met Ali Naqi Khan who impressed him so much, that Wajid Ali later appointed him prime minister of Awadh.

Prime Minister Ali Naqi Khan

Finally, Wajid Ali married Waziran and gave her the title of 'Nigar Mahal'.

As her mother's opposition to this alliance continued, she was arrested on the instructions of Prime Minister Amin-ud-daulah and put in jail for about two or three months, till, on Wajid Ali's instruction, she was released. Wajid Ali tried to persuade Bi Jan to give up her profession, but failed; as a result her daughter, Waziran, also drifted away from her.

A Lucknowi Soap Opera

Nawab Wajid Ali Shah's wife and mother shared a very strained relationship. The reasons for this were as common as in any ordinary household: insecurity, ambition and jealousy. *Begums of Awadh* records about the chief begum of Nawab Wajid Ali Shah, 'It was Khas Mahal who first discourteously hinted to her mother-in-law and her second son that they must meet their own expenses while at Calcutta.' This ugly situation was saved by the Nawab who wisely allocated separate funds for each of them.

Although the chief wife, Nawab Khas Mahal, was the mother of the heir apparent and accordingly given a monthly allowance of Rs 5,000, while the rest of the wives received just Rs 3,000 or less, she failed to get the importance or devotion from her husband that she thought she deserved. Elahi Jan, a palace employee close to the begum, writes that Khas Mahal was not given ceremonial honours and was not considered as significant as her mother-in-law, Malika-i-Kishwar. W.H. Sleeman writes, '[The] mother of the heir apparent was a person of no mark of influence, either in public or private.' Also, the mother-in-law, Malika-i-Kishwar, was quite a popular and dignified lady whose importance the Nawab could not ignore in the administration of the kingdom. He not only respected her, but, to a certain degree, feared her too.

Under such circumstances, a worried Malika-i-Kishwar thought that a frustrated and ambitious Khas Mahal could poison the Nawab to clear the way for her own son's ascension to power. So, to protect the Nawab's life, she got him married off to the eleven-year-old daughter of the minister, Ali Naqi Khan, who was very powerful in the court.

This made the rift between the mother-in-law and the daughter-in-law wider, which lasted till the two women parted ways after the annexation of the kingdom by the British. Malika-i-Kishwar was about to leave for England to plead the case of her son, Nawab Wajid Ali. In the changed situation, Malika-i-Kishwar, who had mellowed with time, thought it wiser to reconciliate with her daughter-in-law before leaving. After an emotional reunion arranged through trusted maids, Malika-Kishwar bid adieu to Nawab Khas Mahal, and left India never to return.

The Faithful Alam Ara

She might not have got along well at times with her husband, Nawab Wajid Ali Shah, but in times of crises, she stood beside him like a rock. Nawab Alam Ara Begum, the chief consort of Wajid Ali Shah, will always be remembered in the history of Lucknow by the gardens Alam Bagh, named after her by Wajid Ali Shah.

The daughter of a respected noble of Delhi, Nawab Ali Khan, she was given the title of 'Azam Babu', but was popularly called 'Nawab Khas Mahal'. She was married to Nawab Wajid Ali Shah in 1838, when he was about fifteen years old. Her doting father-in-law, Nawab Amjad Ali Shah, fixed pin money of four hundred rupees for her personal expenses.

Unfortunately, Khanjar records, Wajid Ali soon fell out with her because of his intrigues with female employees of the palace. This did not come in the way of her being supportive however. When Wajid Ali, after losing his kingdom, went to Calcutta on 13 March 1856 to live like a commoner, she decided to stay by his side. Not only this, in 1857, when Wajid Ali was imprisoned by the British in Fort William in Calcutta, the begum corresponded directly with the British, trying to prove that her husband had not been involved in the Sepoy Mutiny and should be released.

At last, Wajid Ali was set free by the British. Sadly, people with vested interests created a rift between the husband and wife, as a result of which Alam Ara's financial condition deteriorated. She even tried, unsuccessfully, to get a direct pension from the British, similar to the one they had offered Begum Hazrat Mahal and Birjis Qadr.

Alam Ara was an accomplished poet. According to Sheikh Tasadduq Hussain, she wrote a collection of ghazals titled *Beyaz-e-Ishq* (Lover's Diary) and a masnawi titled, *Masnawi-e-Alam*.

Her intellect and intensity can be glimpsed in the following lines she wrote:

Teacher, why do you frighten me with death?

A lover is ne'er afraid to lose his life

Without hope we live in the Garden of World like cypress.

Rich green to the eye no fruit to bear.

This self-respecting begum invariably recommended to her husband a dignified approach while dealing with the British. Once, when the king wrote a qasida (form of poetry) flattering the Governor-General, Lord Canning, Alam Ara initially refused to hand over the royal seal to affix to the poem, on the ground that it was nothing short of disguised begging. The king, however, paid no heed to her.

Nawab Khas Mahal passed away on 13 March 1897, in Matia Burj, Calcutta.

How Wajid Ali Organised his Harem

The last Nawab of Awadh, Wajid Ali Shah, had a large number of wives in his harem. Michael Edwardes in his book *Red Year*, mentions: 'A girl usually enters as Khawasin or attendant. If the King liked her, she was promoted as Pari or dancing girl. If she were taken into concubinage, she became begum. Ultimately, if fortunate enough to have a child by the King, her name was changed', — the word 'Mahal' was added to her name — and she was usually given a separate palace to live in.

In the book *Bannee* (Bride) written by the Nawab himself in 1875, he admits to having 217 wives in his harem. Out of these wives, forty-seven were mahal, thirty-two begum, four munta'ai, and rest of them from other categories. The Arabic word 'muta' means enjoyment; thus, a Muta marriage indicates a marriage contract for a limited period, usually for some monetary consideration. Women married under this arrangement were called mumtu'a or muta'ai. Nawabs had a long tradition of Muta'ai marriages, because it was convenient and had religious sanction.

According to Tasadduq Hussain, at the time of Wajid Ali's death on 21 September 1887, he had 250 Muta'ai wives, excluding the Nikhai wives. Muta'ai wives were further classified into different categories and their monthly allowances ranged between Rs 15 to 150 per month. The categories included khilwatian, wives who performed menial services, well-known among them were Abdar Jan, Amani and Musaffa Begum; childless wives, like Mahru Begum, Chundri Begum and Afzal Begum; at the top of the hierarchy were the mothers of his children, like Mumtaz Mahal, Ulfat Mahal and Nazuk Mahal.

No one could ever doubt Wajid Ali's organisational skills.

The Dastardly Acts of the Nawabs

The weakness that the Nawabs of Lucknow had for women was legendary. And, because they were used to having their every whim catered to, they did not hestitate to stoop to low levels to attain a woman they were interested in.

The third Nawab of Awadh, Shuja-ud-daulah, began showing his weakness for women from a very young age. Once, in the very beginning of his reign, he almost lost his kingdom because of this weakness. According to the scholar Amir Hasan, 'Shuja-ud-daulah caused wide spread resentment among the Khateries by abducting an eighteen-year-old Khatri damsel for a night of love, and some Mughal nobles plotted to replace him.'

Other writers too have described this incident in which, with the help of two Naga brothers, Himmat Bahadur and Umrao Giri, Shuja-ud-daulah kidnapped a girl, unknowingly putting his kingdom at stake. According to *Begums of Awadh*, 'Soon after his accession to the masnad, and being free of his mother's surveillance, he plunged into endless debauchery and other vices. Smitten by the charm of an eighteen-year-old Khatri girl at Ayodhya, he is supposed to have abducted her for one night.' Enraged, but helpless against the power of the ruler, her family members lodged a complaint with Diwan Raja Ram Narayan. Not only this, a big group of Khatries met Ismail Beg Khan, one of the loyal lieutenants of Safdar Jung, to protest.

According to Imad-us-Saadat, the army and Ismail Beg Khan, who had their own reasons to remove Shuja-ud-daulah, took the decision to punish the Naga brothers and ask the Nawab not to deal with them anymore. It was also decided that, if the Nawab failed to act according to their wish, they would call Muhammad Quli Khan of Allahabad to come and take over the masnad. And

Nawab Shuja-ud-daulah

143

in such a case, the Nawab would be sent to some far-flung jagir.

As expected, the unrepentant Nawab refused to accept their conditions, so the army and Ismail Beg Khan decided to go ahead with their plans to topple him. Fortunately for the Nawab, his mother, Sadr-i-Jahan Begum, who had great influence in the court and was deft in dealing with the courtiers, came to his rescue. She called Raja Ram Narayan and reminded him of his loyalty to the throne from the days of her late husband Nawab Safdar Jung. She told him that she was shocked to know that highly placed people connected with the palace were making such a big issue of an insignificant incident. She did not forget to remind him of the favours her late husband had done for him. A convinced Raja Ram assured her that he would placate the Hindu family, but insisted that she talk to Ismail Beg and other high officials to bring them around.

Sadr-i-Jahan Begum invited all the important officers of the court who could play a decisive role in this case, and reminded them of a long list of reasons why they should remain loyal to her son and to the throne of Awadh. In conclusion, according to *Sawanihat-i-Salatin-i-Awadh*, she said, 'Be true to the salt you have been eating.' At the end of the meeting, she distributed expensive gifts to the officials who were by now more than convinced that it was in their own interest to side with the Nawab. Thus the shrewd Sadr-i-Jahan managed to save her son.

In another instance of a kidnapping, albeit for romantic reasons, the eighth ruler, Nasir-ud-din Haider, who came to the throne on 20 October 1827, once kidnapped a beautiful girl, Qamrchahra. The girl was the adopted daughter of Sarfraz Mahal, the wife of Prince Mirza Sulaiman Shikoh, who lived at Lucknow. The Nawab was so taken with her charm that he sent a proposal of marriage through one Mir Fazal Ali. He even tried to make the Prince agree by offering to increase his allowance by Rs 5,000. Sulaiman Shikoh, knowing the Nawab's nature very well, rejected the proposal. Nasir-ud-din finally decided to have the girl kidnapped. She was brought to the palace of his chief begum, Sultan Bahu, with whom he never got along well. As the *Sawanihat-i-Salatin-Awadh* has it, an annoyed Sulaiman approached the British Resident, who confronted the Nawab. To save face, the Nawab told the Resident that his case had been misrepresented. Mirza Sulaiman Shikoh was so disgusted with this incident that he left Lucknow to live in Kasgunj and Akbarabad.

One of the most cultured and civilised Nawabs of the Awadh dynasty, Wajid Ali Shah, was not above committing this dastardly deed. K.S. Santha records, 'Wajid Ali Shah took vengeance on a village girl for her stubborn refusal to succumb to his will. The fiancé of the girl was trapped and killed.' But at the orders of his mother, Janab-i-Alia Malika-i-Kishwar, the girl was sent back to her village.

The Begum who Ruled Lucknow for a Year

The Nawabs of the Awadh dynasty either ruled Awadh at the discretion of the Mughal Emperors of India or at the mercy of the British in India. But there was one legendary woman from an ordinary family who took control of Lucknow from the British by force and practically ruled it for a year.

This beautiful lady started her career as a member of the famous Pari Khana of Nawab Wajid Ali Shah. When she became pregnant, as per the practice, she was elevated to the status of begum and given the title of 'Iftikharunnisa Begum'.

It is interesting to note that this begum, who won universal adulation for her role in the first war of independence, was one of the eight wives who were once divorced by the superstitious Wajid Ali when he found snake-like marks on their backs. However, they were later taken back into the harem.

There are two different versions on how this wife, who was conferred the title of 'Begum Hazrat Mahal' by Wajid Ali at the time of his coronation, went on to rule Lucknow.

According to a historian of that era, Kamaluddin Haider, Begum Hazrat Mahal's minor son Birjis Qadr was crowned king on 7 July 1857 by freedom fighters on the recommendation of Mammu Jan. As per another version, after the capture of Lucknow, the freedom fighters were looking for a person who would be acceptable to everyone. Ultimately they decided on Wajid Ali's son and, according to Elahi Jan, a palace employee who was very close to the begum, 'they forcibly took away Birjis Qadr despite pleadings and protestation by Hazrat Mahal'.

Historians may offer varying accounts of how Begum Hazrat Mahal's son was crowned, but they all agree that as Birjis Qadr was

Begum Hazrat Mahal

a minor, his mother ended up as the de facto ruler of Lucknow from 7 July 1857 to 16 July 1858. This was the period when she participated in the first freedom struggle against the British rule — the Sepoy Mutiny of 1857. During this time she showed exceptional courage and a tremendous organisational capacity; she brought together people with different points of view and at times with different interests. She was well-loved for the pivotal role she played in the Mutiny. W.H. Russel, in his *My Diary in India in the Year 1885-89,* describing her, says the begum was a better man than her husband.

When the British failed to match Hazrat Mahal's might in battle, they stooped low to tarnish her image. They spread rumours that Birjis Qadr was the son of Mammu Jan. Finally, betrayed by traitors in her camp, Hazrat Mahal lost to the British, and fled to Nepal along with her son. The British tried to tempt her by offering her a pension if she did not claim the throne for her son. But she declined, preferring to live on a meagre pension of Rs 500. The prime minister of Nepal gave her a place to live, and it was in that country that she died in 1879.

The Romantic Life of Wajid Ali Shah

Nawab Wajid Ali Shah's record of his life and the women he had affairs with reveals a dark side of life in the Lucknow palaces. While Wajid Ali Shah was known to have had a weakness for women, records reveals that his first sexual experiences were, in fact, forced on him.

The prince was only eight when he was molested by a forty-five-year old woman, Rahiman, who worked in the palace. Wajid Ali Shah writes that once, while he was sleeping, Rahiman began taking liberties with him. When he tried to ward her off, she threatened to get him punished by his tutor. After that day, she often approached him for sexual gratification and kept on doing so till he was ten years old.

After Rahiman's departure from the scene, a forty-year-old woman, Ameeran, who worked for his mother, began trying to seduce him whenever he was alone in the room. This time, however, Wajid Ali says, he secretly enjoyed it.

After these two forced affairs, he was himself floored by a twenty-three-year-old beauty, Bunno who worked with his mother. This time, it was Wajid Ali who made the advances and it was Bunno who resisted him. However, at a later stage, their relationship became intimate.

By this time, Wajid Ali was ready to get involved with any girl that took his fancy. Bunno had a twenty-two-year-old sister, Hazi Khanam. She was married and had a child, but the prince was so besotted that, despite his parents' opposition, he used to meet her through Immami Khanam, a worker in the palace.

Soon, Immami, who was about forty years old, tried to take the place of Hazi Khanam. Wajid Ali writes that Immami Khanam was an unattractive woman who thought that she was very beautiful. Since she knew his secrets, she tried to take advantage of him. But, the Nawab said, he never gave in to her smooth talk.

The next love interest in the prince's life was a fourteen-year-old girl from Faizabad, Ilahi Khanam. Her feelings for him were probably sincere: while parting, she gave him a ring and two ivory combs as gifts.

Fed up with his romantic pecadillos, his parents got Wajid Ali married off at the age of sixteen to Nawab Khas Mahal. As history went on to show, however, marriage did nothing to stop Wajid Ali Shah's amorous adventures.

The Begums' Revenge

It is but natural that the oppressed invariably strike back at the first available opportunity. Nawab Wajid Ali Shah's experience with his numerous begums was no exception to this rule.

When he was at the best of his health and wealth, Wajid Ali, disregarding the sentiments of his wives, continued to recruit new inmates to his harem from different levels of society. This not only hurt the begums' feelings, but went against their interests. These ageing and neglected begums often, but not always willingly, arranged beautiful girls for the Nawab, hoping to get back in favour with him.

Nawab Wajid Ali writes about his first wife, Alam Ara Begum, with whom he was married at the age of fifteen: 'As she was wise and intelligent, she understood it well that her purpose would not be served unless she obeyed me and carried out my orders. Therefore she started sending me women clandestinely.' The important women, who came into the life of Wajid Ali through Alam Ara, were Shah Bakhsh, Altaf Bakhsh and Wazir Pari.

Other begums too did not lag behind in this race. A good number of his wives were instrumental in arranging beautiful women for Wajid Ali's pleasure. For example, his wife, Nawab Nishat Begum, introduced Amir Pari into his harem.

The begums, who felt forced to undertake this humiliating task for their survival, retaliated when Wajid Ali was afflicted with syphilis. He wrote in his book *Tarkikh-e-Parikhana*: 'During my illness, Mahbooba Alam and Khusru Begum, along with Qaiser Begum, went away to Jalal-ud-daulah House, gifted by me for [their] recreation, and left me in the hands of Hakim. Hidden from me, [they] enjoy the pleasures of the world, and because of my disease I cannot interfere.'

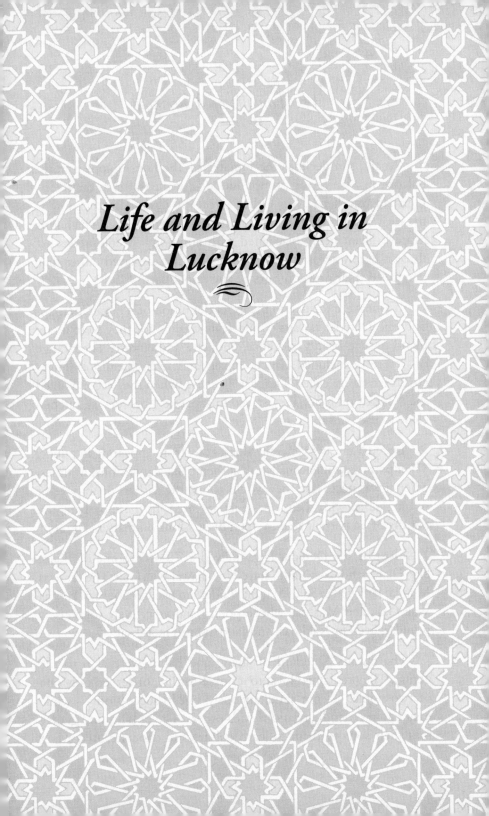

Life and Living in Lucknow

The Tawaifs of Lucknow

'As the sun declines the inmates of the houses appear in the balcony in a variety of groups and look at the traffic in the street,' German traveller L.Von Orlich wrote of tawaifs in Lucknow in the early nineteenth century. '…they have piercing eyes which look more brilliant being blackened with antimony. A coloured scarf thrown lightly across the neck and shoulder displayed rather than concealed their fine contours of the upper part.'

If one were to stick to the exact definition of a tawaif, perhaps only the Deredar tawaifs would truly qualify, for they were a rare blend of wit, beauty, elegance, etiquette and culture. Their range of interests included dance, music and even literature. These courtesans were called 'Deredar' because, when they accompanied the Nawabs on tours, they stayed in separate tents (deras), pitched close to the Nawab's tents.

Deredar tawaifs generally shied away from appearing in public. Their patrons would usually call at their palatial mansions. At times, when it was necessary, they would attend the darbars of important nobles, albeit with their faces fully covered. In these darbars, the tawaifs often participated in open discussions on matters literary.

Most of the Deredar tawaifs lived in Chowk. Some of them, like Allah Bandi and Najju, stayed in Chawal Wali Gali. The famous Mughal Jan lived in Sabji Mandi; Haider Jan had her house in Parcha Wali Gali; and Mushtri, whose poetry and voice were immensely popular, lived in Nakkhas; and Jaddan lived in Taksal.

The tawaifs' standard of living and habits were akin to the gentry. They remained loyal to a noble for life, or served only one or two nobles — not simultaneously, but in succession — while maintaining friendly relations with others. The nobility and gentry sent their sons to them to learn culture and etiquette. According to writer Mirza Jafar Hussain, he too was sent to learn tehzeeb, etiquette, from the famous tawaifs Nanhua and Bachua.

Their style of living, and even the decoration of their houses, followed a set pattern. There was always a separate sitting room, decorated with chandeliers, candlestands and coloured bulbs. Seating was arranged on the floor or a takht (wooden bed), covered with carpets and rugs. There were masnads against which people could lean.

The tawaifs usually wore an angiya, which was made of a thin cloth; a kurti or shaluka was worn over a kalidar painch made of twelve yards of cloth. Their dupattas usually had kamdani work. Sarees only became popular in the later years.

The Deredar tawaifs were well organised and even had their own panchayat. Virginity was given as much importance among the prostitutes as among the gentry for the simple reason that it meant good business. The sale of virginity through auction was a lucrative business. The following deflowering ceremony — euphemistically known as 'nath utarna', meaning 'taking off the nose ring' — was celebrated with much pomp and show. The Deredar courtesans called this ceremony 'missi' and celebrated it with the same elaborate arrangements that a marriage required. Friends, relatives and patrons came from far and wide to attend it. The house was decorated, and singers and dancers were called from far off places. The expenses for all these festivities were borne by the client.

At the end, the girl, dressed like a bride, was sent into a specially decorated room, to meet the client, the highest bidder.

The practice was that, later, the initiated girl remained in the service of her first client for a stipulated period of time. She received an allowance from him during this period. For example, girls from the Chaudharain community claimed Rs 1,000 per month in those days.

Cult of the Courtesans

The courtesans of Awadh were not only instrumental in moulding Lucknow's cultural milieu, they were also key players in the political set-up throughout the 135 years of Nawabi rule.

While history recounts many such instances, a notable example was that of the beautiful Piyaju, who had emptied her coffers to boost the career of Hakim Mehdi Ali Khan, prime minister of Nawab Nasir-ud-din Haider. The most famous of all, however, was Mahak Pari, who fought for the country's freedom and has now been immortalised in history as Begum Hazrat Mahal. Another courtesan, Husaini, who was often called to the Residency to perform mujras for the burra sahibs of the East India Company, later became the most favoured wife of Nasir-ud-din Haider.

The tawaif culture emerged in 1754, when Shuja-ud-daula became the ruler. Declining fortunes of the Mughal Empire witnessed almost a mass exodus of nautch girls from Delhi to Faizabad.

Mohammed Faiz Baksh, in his book *Tarrikh-e-Farahbaksh,* wrote that Shuja-ud-daula was accompanied by hundreds of women on tour, who had mastered the art of music and dance. The nobles soon followed suit, and began taking a retinue of their favoured tawaifs on tours. Many courtesans accompanied the Nawab and lived in stately, specially-pitched tents near the Nawab's camp.

Asif-ud-daulah was a step ahead of his father when it came to a fondness for women. While Bari Misri was undoubtedly his favourite, others who entertained his court were Salaro, Ram Kali, Hirajan, Jalalo, and Khursheed Jan.

It is said that Wajid Ali Shah suffered from palpitations of heart, so under medical advice he engaged beautiful women for his amusement. Among them, Chhuttan and Hassan Bandi carved a niche for themselves. Young tawaif Waziran's charm enamoured Wajid Ali Shah so much that, when her mother Bi Jan refused to send her daughter to him, he threatened to shoot himself with a pistol.

It has been observed that, in the early twentieth century, a majority of tawaifs were Muslims. The explanation given was that most of them were originally Hindus from lower castes who, in order to improve their social status, embraced Islam and became Shia Muslims.

According to Abdul Halim Sharar, a famous journalist and the author of *Guzishta Lukhnau*, the courtesans of Lucknow could be divided into different categories. First, there were the Kanchani, of the Kanchan tribe, who had migrated from Punjab and Delhi and were professional harlots. The second category was the Chunna Wallis, originally lime sellers who got into prostitution. Chunna Wali Haideri, the legendary singer, came from this community. Hundreds of people waited for hours at her Imambara to listen to her soz recitals. Then there were the Nagrant, who came from Gujarat and were professional prostitutes.

Another category was that of the Takiyas, who lived in areas around Chowk, Akbari Gate and Chawal Walli Gali. Their clientele comprised the economically and socially lower classes, and they were therefore not allowed to operate from Chowk. Owing to their formal training in dance and music, Randis were more acceptable to the Nawabs than the Takiyas. Even poets and men of letters did not mind patronising the former. The Randis' domicile was in the heart of Chowk.

The last two types of courtesans operated openly. The Khangis on the whole lived a normal life with their families, and clandestinely did business on the side. Nawab Wajid Ali Shah himself mentioned in his accounts that Begum Hazrat Mahal was a Khangi.

The most popular, accepted and even respected class of courtesans was the Deredar, also called Derewali, tawaifs. They got this name from the many tents they owned; the tents, which cost a fortune, were necessary for their peripatetic lifestyle. They were direct descendants of the courtesans of the Mughal court.

The Nawab and the Djinns

The people of Awadh — across all castes and religions — were particularly superstitious. Hindu Malis were called by Muslims to perform pujas to cure smallpox cases, and it was not uncommon to find Hindus wearing charms and talismans given by Maulvis to ward off evil spirits.

Towards the end of Amjad Ali's reign, a commoner, Razi-ud-daulah Qutb-ud-daulah, became a power to reckon with by virtue of being the brother of the king's latest muse, Amman, also known by the title 'Suroor Jahan'.

In order to bring Razi-ud-daulah down in the king's eyes, the king's Wazir, Nawab Imdad Husain, conspired with a courtesan, Ashfaqul Sultan, who bore enmity with him. It was decided that they would declare him the 'king of djinns'. They roped in one of the king's old and trusted informers inside the palace, Ustani, to 'confidentially reveal' the supernatural powers of djinns to the king. Amjad Ali trusted Ustani completely and was very impressed by her revelations. The Wazir's plans, however, came to a standstill when Amjad Ali suddenly died on 13 February 1847.

Later, after Wajid Ali Shah ascended the throne, Razi-ud-daulah — who was by now aware of the rumours associating him with djinns — decided to use it to his advantage. With great care, a house was specifically renovated and remodelled to accommodate many passages and exits. Here, in a ghostlike atmosphere, a 'meeting' was arranged between the Nawab and the djinns. Wajid Ali was completely won over, and from then, the 'djinns' began giving him advice that favoured Razi-ud-daulah, and discredited his enemies.

But this could not last long. One day, the same courtesan who had conspired to create this farce, Ashfaqul Sultan, exposed the plot to the Nawab. According to Sheikh Tasaddq Husain, as a result Razi-ud-daulah, his family and co-conspirators were all jailed.

The Bridegroom's Jewellery

No Oriental king ever lived more luxuriously then Nawab Asif-ud-daulah. The marriage of his son, Wazir Ali, was celebrated with a grandiosity that even the great Mughals would have been hard pressed to surpass, remarks historian J. Pemble.

A Britisher invited to the wedding has been quoted in both the *Asiatic Annual Register* and *The History of Asif-ud-ulla* as saying that the marriage procession had about 1,200 richly caparisoned elephants, 100 of which had howdahs covered with silver; Nawab Asif-ud-daulah himself sat on an exceptionally big elephant, which was covered with gold cloth, and his howdah was studded with precious stones.

The description goes on to say: 'On both sides of the road on which the procession was moving artificial minarets made of bamboo were erected and these were covered with lights in lamps. On each side of our procession, richly dressed dancing girls and musicians were carried on moving platforms covered with gold and silver cloth and supported by the bearer. There were two dancing girls and two musicians on each platform and the number of such platforms was about 100 on each side.

'On the entire route, firework of high quality was displayed. There was a large edifice in the centre of the garden where we reached and here we were introduced into a grand saloon adorned with innumerable girandoles and pendant lusters of English manufacture, lit with candles. Here while we had sumptuous European and native food with all kind of fruits, sweetmeats and wine, about a hundred girls sang and danced their native dances.'

The festivity continued for three successive nights. It is mentioned that in this most expensive marriage of its time (it cost more than $300,000), the bridegroom, Wazir Ali, was wearing so much jewellery, he could scarcely walk properly, staggering under the weight of precious stones and metals.

Legend has it that the ruler of Kashmir too came to Lucknow, with his staff, to attend the wedding. It said that the group was so impressed by Lucknow, several of them decided to stay on permanently; they settled in localities like Katra Abu Tarab and Rustam Nagar. These immigrants included both Hindus and Muslims. While the Muslims were mostly musicians and craftsmen, the Hindu settlers later produced poets, lawyers and educationists.

Cockfights in Lucknow

Cockfighting was a very popular form of entertainment in the Nawabi period. The importance attached to these fights can be gauged by the fact that when the famous poet, Mir Taqui Mir, visited Lucknow on Nawab Asif-ud-daulah's invitation, his first meeting with the Nawab was arranged during a cockfight.

Royal patronage for this game can be traced to the third Nawab, Shuja-ud-daulah, and his descendants continued to support the tradition enthusiastically. For example, Nawab Nasiruddin Haidar's roosters fought with those of Major Soirisse and Haidar Beg Khan. Aristocrats were very fond of this game as well: one Agha Budr-ud-din Haidar had more than two hundred birds for this purpose, and a staff of around a dozen men to look after these birds.

It is said that Nawab Saadat Ali Khan often lost a lot of money to a Frenchman, General Claude Martin, settled in Lucknow.

Nawab Wajid Ali Shah carried the tradition with him when he moved to Matia Burj in Calcutta after losing his kingdom. At that time, Nawab Ali Naqui's place was so popular for cockfights, even some Britishers from Calcutta participated in it with their roosters.

These birds were trained with great care and patience. In fact, it was almost seen as a field of specialisation. Usually, a trainer's job started with the selection of the breed, as it played a very important role in the long run. A particular breed, known as Asil and believed to be from West Asia, was much in demand for its fighting spirit. It was observed that birds of this breed had a tendency to fight till death, rather than flee from the scene.

The next important thing was the food for the birds and upkeep of the bird coop. Keepers were also involved with the exercise and

Royal Cockfight

massaging of the roosters. The massaging of limbs was seen as very important, and keepers evolved different massage techniques. Apart from this, since a rooster's beak was an important weapon in a fight, trainers often fed the roosters by hand to avoid any damage to their beak while pecking food from a hard surface.

While preparing for a fight, some trainers would use a knife to scrape the beak of the rooster to sharpen it, thereby making it a more potent weapon. Before the start of a fight, the claws of the roosters were tied to avoid any major injuries.

Once the birds were released for a fight, the owners encouraged their rooster to attack first since this was considered a winning strategy. Cockfights in Lucknow often stretched to several rounds, at times lasting for days together. When the fight reached a point where both the owners realised that the birds were tired and injured and would not be able to provide enough entertainment to the spectators, the fight would be suspended by mutual agreement. This was known as paani, which, in the local language, means water. During this time keepers nursed the birds' wounds by cleaning them with water and prepared them for the next round.

At the end of long-drawn out rounds, the verdict was reached against the rooster which was too injured to put up a strong fight.

Poet Mir Taqui Mir, who was introduced to Asif-ud-daulah during a cockfight

Muslims Celebrated Holi, Hindus Observed Muharram

The Shia Nawabs, who ruled from 1722 to 1856, were ambassadors of communal harmony. Consecutive Nawabs, through force of their character, evolved a culture which brought the Hindu and the Muslim communities closer. As a result, both participated in each other's festivals.

The fourth Nawab, Asif-ud-daulah, and the sixth, Nawab Saadat Ali Khan, and even Prince Suleman, a relative of the Emperor who had migrated to Lucknow, celebrated Holi as state festivals.

Dr Safdar Husani writes in his book *Lucknow ki Tahzibi Miras*, that Asif-ud-daulah spent Rs 5 lakhs in the month of Phagun, on Holi. It is said he followed quite a few of the prevalent rituals of Holi, such as Swang, wherein dances and fireworks were organised on a grand scale. A contemporary poet, Mirza Quateel, says in his book *Haft Tamasha* that on Holi, a fancy dress show would be organised, in which women of the palace enacted the role of Mughal men, greengrocers, recluses, and English-spouting Europeans. At times they mimicked a tiger's roar, as they chased after men.

According to Dr Mohammad Umar's renowned work, *Hindustani Tahzib ka Mussalmano Pe Asar*, Muslims also celebrated Diwali. Many people indulged in gambling and almost everyone lit earthen lamps and bought sugar toys. Not doing so was considered inauspicious.

In this liberal religious social set-up, Hindus too responded with zeal. A good number of them observed Muharram and built Imambaras. Raja Tikait Rai, Raja Mehra and Raja Mewa Ram constructed Imambaras at different places. A Hindu officer, Jhau Lal, built an impressive Imambara in Nawabganj locality.

In those days, Tazia-Dars (keepers of Tazia) could be from any community. Among the Hindu Tazia-Dars, some wore turbans and a tapka (a cloth belt). They did not participate in the recitation of Nauhas (mourning songs or verse) or breast-beating, but would join in the Persian chants.

A Fatwa for Communal Harmony

In the days of Nawab Wajid Ali Shah, a man named Shah Ghulam Hussain from the Hyderabadi locality of Lucknow, declared jihad to take possession of and reconstruct a mosque at the disputed site of Faizabad. Clashes between Muslims and Hindus ensued, and Ali Naqui Khan — Wajid Ali Shah's minister — sent Nazim Agha Ali Khan, Captain Alexander Orr and Raja Man Singh to Ayodhya to mediate between the communities. Eventually, a mutually acceptable compromise was reached.

However, some mischief-mongers — purportedly at the instance of the British Resident, General James Outram — continued to create trouble. In Lucknow, Maulvi Ameer Ali from Amethi and Maulvi Abdur Razzaq of Firangi Mahal raised the Muhammadi Jhanda (The Prophet's standard, religious flag) and declared jihad over the issue.

Ali Naqui Khan personally made efforts, through a relative of Maulvi Ameer Ali to dissuade him in his attempt, but failed. Ameer Ali left for Ayodhya with seventy of his followers. The minister once again tried to defuse the situation by sending Meer Safdar and Ramzan Ali Khan to talk to the Maulvi, but Ameer Ali, according to author Najmul Ghani, arrested both of them. At this, the king's troops surrounded the fortress of Satrikh where Ameer Ali had taken refuge. Ameer Ali was forced to flee to Dariyabad. Interestingly, a group of Maulvis, who had initially backed the jihad at Sandila, went to Ameer Ali and tried to convince him to recall the jihad, but failed. After this, according to the *Hadeeqa-e-Shuhada,* a team of twenty-one Maulvis under Maulvi Saadullah was deputed to convince Ameer Ali, but they too failed.

Disappointed with Ameer Ali, learned Sunni and Shia Maulvis issued a fatwa against his jihad. The Sunni fatwa declared that, so long as the king or the ruler did not give permission, the people had no right to declare jihad on their own. The Shia Ulama in their fatwa said that jihad was not permissible in the absence of the higher authority of an Imam.

The Chef and the Prime Minister

Nawab Ghazi-ud-din Haider, who ruled between 1814 and 1827, was inordinately fond of eating parathas. His chef cooked six parathas for him every day, for which purpose he was given thirty seer of ghee per day; the chef would use about five seer of ghee per paratha.

Once, the Nawab's prime minister, Motamaddaula Agha Mir, asked the chef what he did with thirty seer of ghee. The chef replied, 'I prepare parathas.' The minister said: 'Fine, prepare one in front of me.' The chef prepared six parathas in his presence by using all the ghee; the ghee remaining in the pan was thrown in the drain. When the minister asked for an explanation for this, he replied that the remaining ghee was no longer ghee, but had become oil that was not fit for use. Not satisfied with his answer, Motamaddaula ordered that henceforth the chef be issued only one seer of ghee per paratha.

The chef, not too pleased with such interference, started sending very ordinary parathas to the Nawab. After a few days, the Nawab asked the chef why the quality of the parathas had become so poor. The chef replied that he was following the prime minister's orders, and narrated the entire sequence of events to the king.

Nawab Ghazi-ud-din Haider immediately sent for the prime minister, who tried to convince the king that the chef was cheating him. In reply, the king slapped the prime minister and said: 'Are you not looting the entire estate? Have you ever thought of it? If these people are taking a bit of extra ghee, and that especially for my food, why should you prevent it?'

The prime minister was finally spared only after he apologised by touching both his ears — a gesture of extreme penitence and respect.

Motamaddaula never interfered with the chef's style of working again.

A Chef's Pride is Hurt

The chefs who worked in the Nawabs' kitchens were not only skilled and innovative, they were also very proud of what they considered their art.

Once, a chef who was about to join Nawab Asif-ud-daulah's service was brought in front of the Nawab. Asif-ud-daulah asked him what he could cook, to which he replied, 'I only cook urad ki dal.' When asked how much salary he wanted, he said, 'Rs 500 per month,' which was a fortune in those days. He also had two conditions which he wanted accepted before he started work: whenever the Nawab wanted to eat the dal, he would need to inform the chef a day in advance. The second condition was that when the Nawab was informed that the dish was ready, he would have to eat it without any delay. Both the conditions were accepted, and the time soon came when he was ordered to show his expertise with urad ki dal, dal made from urad lentils.

Accordingly, having made elaborate arrangements, he cooked the lentils and sent a message to the Nawab, that the dal was ready. The Nawab asked the chef to arrange for the dastarkhan to be spread out. However, since he was engaged in a conversation at the time, he soon forgot about the meal. After sometime, the chef informed him that the food was ready; again the Nawab continued with his conversation. When, even after the third reminder, the Nawab did not turn up to eat, the chef simply picked up the vessel containing the dal and emptied it at the base of a tree that was dead. He left immediately after, without informing anyone.

The Nawab felt remorseful, and asked his men to find and bring the chef back, but they could not trace his whereabouts.

After sometime, to everyone's surprise, it was observed that the same dead tree, at the base of which the chef had thrown the dal, had become green and showed signs of growing.

Wajid Ali Shah Plays Lord Krishna

No matter how Nawab Wajid Ali Shah is interpreted by different historians, even his most sever critics cannot deny that he was truly secular. For this most culturally evolved Nawab of Awadh, the artist in him had risen above all religious or sectarian considerations.

Inspired by the traditional romantic play, *Hindu Rahasya*, which revolves around Lord Krishna and his numerous love-struck gopis, Wajid Ali Shah had a play scripted by Amanat Ali, called *Indersabha*.

Once a year, the Nawab organised a play at Kaiserbagh, where he would play the lead role of Lord Krishna; the women of his palace and Pari Khana played the roles of the gopis.

At times, the king enacted the role of a Hindu sadhu. The role required him to cover his entire body with ash, to convey detachment from the world, so the king had a special kind of ash prepared — from burning pearls. Even the make-belief asceticism of the king betrayed the Nawabi opulence!

The plays were occasions for gaiety and merriment. Even the commoners were welcome, and age was no bar. There was, however, one interesting condition: everyone coming to participate in the fair had to dress in ochre only — a colour that is associated with the Hindu religion. The dress code added to the sense of revelry: men dressed up in the spirit of the plays they had come to watch.

Once, when at Matia Burj, a Shia and a Sunni man had a quarrel over some trifling subject. Wajid Ali threw the two men out of the palace, saying Shias and Sunnis were like his two eyes. Is there any better example of secularity than this?

Did the King only Dance with the Barber?

The Nawabs, by and large, were extremely self-indulgent. And anyone who supported and participated in their extravagance wielded considerable influence over them. No one understood this better than the wife of the British Resident Mordaunt Ricketts, who started flirting with the young and youthful Nawab Nasir-ud-din Haider. It is believed that, in the process, she profited handsomely from the gifts and favours she received. To further her interest, in the year 1831, she, through her husband, managed to plant a British barber, who had come to India as cabin boy, in the king's court.

The barber's name was George Derusett and he was employed on the monthly salary of three hundred rupees per month. Derusett succeeded in winning the confidence of the king by catering to his penchant for European hairstyles. Soon, this shrewd barber saw the opportunity to amass more money. He started stoking the Nawab's appetite for wine, women and buffoonery. His flattery knew no limits. Once, to please Nasir-ud-din, he tied both the ends of his uncle's moustaches with twine to his chair. And later, to amuse the king further, he let off fireworks under his uncle's nose in the court and made fun of him in front of everyone.

At another occasion, Derusett, merely for the entertainment of the king, forced the old uncle to get drunk, and then made him dance. The uncle was whirled round by Derusett and his friends till he could barely stand. At last, his turban was knocked off and his clothes were snatched away garment by garment.

Derusett also introduced a beautiful English girl, Miss Walters, to the Nawab, who married her and gave her the title of 'Muqader Alia'.

For rendering these kinds of services, Derusett became Nawab

Nasir-ud-din's favourite and confidant. The relationship of trust and loyalty between the king and Derusett was such that the barber first tasted the wine meant for the king; only then was it served to the king.

Leaving his basic duties far behind, the trusted barber-turned-confidant now acquired the role of constant companion and counsellor to the king. Nawab Nasir-ud-din gave the title of 'Sarfaraz Khan' to this barber and appointed him his advisor. This gave Derusett enough opportunity to mint money as he had direct or indirect say in every decision the king made. He took a commission on the purchase of the goods that he bought for the king from Calcutta and other places.

Derusett's clout increased every day, and the other courtiers were in awe of him. He was seen with Nawab Nasir-ud-din everywhere, even at odd hours. Their close relationship gave rise to suspicions. A report of the disgusted Resident in 1837 says: 'Not only the King's private servants but eighteen or twenty Indo-Britons, composing the King's English band, have several time seen His Majesty dancing country dances as the partner of Mr Derusett, the latter after some grotesque masquerade fashion, and His Majesty attired in the dress of an European lady'. The British Resident further reported darkly of other 'most shocking indecencies'.

As for Nasir-ud-din's unconditional trust in the barber, one is forced to think that the king may have been right. Within four months of the barber's departure from the court, Nasir-ud-din was poisoned. He is buried near the Daliganj railway station at Lucknow.

Pigeons and Parrots

The royals enjoyed and patronised pigeon-fancying. So important was this activity to the Nawabs, that the third Nawab of Awadh, Shuja-ud-daulah, appointed an expert pigeon-fancier, Saiyyid Mir Ali from Bareilly, in his court on very lucrative terms.

Among the other Nawabs who took a special interest in this sport, were the founder of Chowk, Asif-ud-daulah; the Nawab who had given half of his kingdom to the British, Saadat Ali Khan; the first king of Awadh, Ghazi-ud-din Haider; and his son Nawab Nasir-ud-din Haider. The last Nawab, Wajid Ali Shah, was so fond of pigeons, once while at Calcutta, he bought a pair of silk-winged pigeons for Rs 25,000. At the time of his death, he had about twenty-four thousand pigeons which were managed by a team of keepers under the supervision of famous pigeon expert, Ghulam Abbas.

Encouraged by the royal patronage, bird experts in Lucknow were spurred to excellence in training pigeons. They attached a lot of importance to pigeon breeding. Their preferred varieties were Lotan, Shiraz, Guli, Laqqa, Peshawari, Girah Baz and Goley. This last category had the tendency to bring back the pigeons of competitor pigeon-keepers and increase its owner's stock.

One expert during the reign of Nasir-ud-din Haidar had a particular trick that was so popular, people paid him five rupees to perform it in their house. This trainer would go to the person's house with his pigeon cage and release his pigeons there. Once the birds flew away, he would whistle, at the sound of which the pigeons would come from wherever they were to that very house and fly back into their cage.

Another expert, Nawab Paley, had trained his pigeons to perform, at the sound of his whistle, different acts, including somersaults, in the air. One Mir Aman Ali was known for producing pigeons of a desired colour by plucking out the feathers of a bird and replacing them with coloured feathers in the same apertures. Rich people bought his pigeons for as much as twenty rupees.

One expert even managed to train parrots to behave like pigeons. In the evening, Mir Muhammad Ali would come to the Hussainabad area with his set of a dozen parrots and release them from their cage. After sometime, at the signal of his whistle, they would descend and, like pigeons, go back into their cage.

The Great Storytellers

Storytelling has been the main source of entertainment through the ages all over the world. In Nawabi Lucknow, storytellers enjoyed a special status. Legendary storytellers contributed a great deal to the development of spoken Urdu, and later on, influenced even the written Urdu of Lucknow by their impressive vocabulary, style and eloquence.

Like courtesans and poets, early storytellers too migrated to Lucknow from Delhi. They were given so much importance they decided to make Lucknow their permanent home. These storytellers were a combination of different talents: apart from the fertile imagination and mastery over the language they share with today's fiction writers, they also had the unique ability to change the story line, at the demand of the listener, in the middle of a narration. They were intelligent enough to choose and use words according to the mental level of different assemblies of listeners. Not only this, they were excellent performers too. Their pronunciation, modulation of emotive voice and vocabulary gave such a graphic description of events, that the audience sat listening for hours on end.

Listening to stories became such a popular pastime that, from the rich to the poor, all kinds of people were engulfed by this passion. Nawabs and other rich people had their own personal storytellers. There were also female storytellers, and they were employed in the harems to entertain the royal ladies.

Ordinary people gathered in the market place, like the Chowk, to listen to stories and pay whatever they could afford to, as they did and still do to the acrobats or naqqals performing on the streets. It has been said that the opium addicts of Lucknow became addicted to listening to stories too, for this was their main pastime.

The themes of the stories largely fell under categories like love, beauty, pleasure, deception, and war. In fact, most of the stories had their plots and characters directly or indirectly woven around the famous Persian work *Dastan-e-Amir-Hamza*. This book — which revolves around the adventures of the protagonist, Amir Hamza, and his encounters with devils, fairies, charms and magic — is believed to have been composed by Abdul Hasan Amir Khusrau (1255–1325).

Amir Khusrau is one of the most admired persons in Indian history. He was a reputed scholar, Sufi saint, soldier, musician and poet. He served in the court of Muhammad Tughlaq. *Dastan-e-Amir-Hamza* is about 18,000-pages long, and was published in separate volumes. The book that the modern reader identifies as *Dastan-e-Amir-Hamza* is assumed to have been the work of Faizi, who probably retold it to entertain Emperor Akbar.

The everlasting impact of these great storytellers of Lucknow can be clearly seen in the early works in Urdu including *Bostan-e-Khayal*, translated by Mir Taqi Khayal; *Tilism-e-Hosh Ruba*, translated by Mir Muhammad Husain Jah and Ahmad Husain Qamar; and *Nausherwan-Nama*, translated by Tassaduq Husain from Persian.

The Roots of Lucknow's Carefree Attitude

Culture and commerce always flourish when political stability reigns. Such conditions were created in Lucknow when the British alliance gave the city a guarantee of security. This is the reason why Lucknow, one of the major cities in Northern India, never needed to be walled. The Nawabs and the rest of the aristocracy diverted the material resources and time, saved from the destruction and vagaries of war, to the field of art and culture.

The revenue collected in the Nawabs' Lucknow, was considerably higher in comparison to that collected in other places in the Mughal Empire. Revenue was gained from the taxes on markets, roads, pilgrims and customs duties, but their main source was land revenue from the fertile rural areas of Awadh. According to Safi Ahmad, in the year 1844–45 (during the rule of Amjad Ali Shah), the land revenue was about 1.6 crores of rupees.

Most of this income was spent in Lucknow by the Nawabs, except a meagre sum that went to pay pensions and salaries to civil servants and soldiers from rural areas or for importing goods. Even highly-paid people, who were attached to the court, spent all their money in Lucknow. For example, Nawab Nasir-ud-din Haider's prime minister, Roshan-ud-daulah, received a salary of Rs 25,000 a month, plus a five percent commission on the total collection of revenue, which came to around Rs 6 lakh. Apart from this, a sum of Rs 5 lakh per year from the royal coffers took care of the monthly allowances of his two wives and son. Thus his annual income was in the range of Rs 15 lakh.

Lucknow had no industries in those days, except cottage and handicraft. The aristocracy in Lucknow loved to live in style, and had a lot of money at their disposal. So, it was but natural that, finding no other options, they spent most of their money on a train of servants, courtesans, entertainers, cockfights, kite flying and purchases in Lucknow. W.H. Sleeman may have been right when he said, '[the] ruler(s) of Awadh spend all they can spare for the public in gratifying the vitiated tastes of the overgrown metropolis'.

An interesting fact is that, while people living in rural areas worked hard to pay taxes, the common people living in Lucknow, paid almost no taxes. It was not surprising then, that Lucknowites developed a strong liking for the Nawabs of Awadh.

When money started freely flowing from the top to the lower level of society, people became used to an easy way of life. They began paying more attention to the finer things of life; they concentrated on acquiring mannerisms and proper etiquette, rather than working hard. This gradually changed the mindset of the people of Lucknow, as its famed easy-going culture set in for all time to come.

The Prince of Wales and the Nawab

In 1876, the Prince of Wales, along with Lord Beaconsfield, visited India. He held a durbar at Calcutta that was attended by the royal families of India.

When the raja of Benaras, Ishri Prasad Narayan Singh, arrived in Calcutta to attend the durbar, he sent a message through S. Ameer Ali — a close confidante of the king — seeking audience with Nawab Wajid Ali. 'I still consider the King as my real master,' the message stated, 'and I will feel highly gratified if I am admitted in his presence. I have also a few precious gems worthy of Kings, which I wish to offer him as nazar.'

To Ameer Ali' surprise, Wajid Ali turned down the request and ordered that, as per earlier customs, the minister Wazeer-us-Sultan would meet the raja.

Ameer Ali conveyed the message to Narayan Singh, who was very disappointed. When Wajid Ali was told about this, he said: 'You told me [the Raja] wanted to gift me some very precious jewels. Had I accepted this costly nazar [gift] from him, I [would than] have [to], in turn [give] him a costlier gift. But what do I have to give him? So, it is better I should not see him at all.'

Wajid Ali chose not to attend the durbar. When he was informed that the prince was keen on meeting him, the self-respecting Wajid Ali sent this message: 'If you consider me to be a king, then it is below my status to go to you. But if in your eyes I am a homeless beggar, then how dare I face you?'

This candid reply had the desired effect on the prince, who then came to meet the Nawab at Matia Burj. While parting, despite his financial crisis, the king presented the prince a walking stick studded with diamonds and pearls.

A Courtesan for Ransom

In the days of Nawab Ghazi-ud-din Haidar, a man, Sayid Mohammad Isa Mian, alias Isa Mian, for whose arrest the British had announced the prize of Rs 2,000, lived in the guise of a fakir in Lucknow. According to the British, he was an accused in the Bareilly riots, or the revolt of April 1816, in which many lives were lost. He was also the main accused in a murder.

On the recommendation of one Fakir Mohammad Khan Risaldar, Isa Mian got in touch with the prime minister Agha Mir and became close to him. Unfortunately, this familiarity proved to be costly for Agha Mir.

Isa Mian was having an affair with a charming courtesan named Mussamat Bibi Jan. The love affair was bound to end, however, because of his harsh behaviour. One day the courtesan fled from the house and went to the prime minister's wife, to seek sanctuary. The sympathetic begum took Bibi Jan under her protection and allowed her to live in the palace.

Isa Mian, confident of his friendship with Agha Mir, asked him to send Bibi Jan back to him. Agha Mir refused on the grounds that she was not married to Isa Mian and, as such, was free to go anywhere. Isa Mian then approached the teacher of the prime minister's sons, Maulvi Karamat Ali, but he too declined to help him, stating the same reason. Isa Mian, who took this as a personal insult, decided to settle the issue in his own manner.

He conspired with some antisocial elements of Lucknow, and with their help, on 2 June 1824, raided the place where Agha Mir's two sons, the six-year-old Nizam-ud-daulah and the eleven-year-old Agha Ali, were taking tuition. It was around six in the morning, and Agha Mir had gone to meet Nawab Ghazi-ud-din; Maulvi Karamat Ali was in the bathroom, while his assistant, Maulvi Ameeen Ali, was giving lessons to the two boys in the maktab, the place of study.

Isa Mian's entry, with one servant and six armed men into the maktab, was quite dramatic. First he formally greeted the children and complimented them for the progress they were making in their studies. With this, the six armed men whipped out their firearms and covered all the three doors in the maktab. After this, at a signal, eight armed men barged into the room; two of them, carrying kataars (small swords), grabbed the boys and told them if they tried to run away or shouted they would be killed.

By this time, quite a few important people like Khas Mahal Nazir Ali Khan's son-in-law, Roshan-ud-daulah, Subhan Ali Khan, and Fakir Mohammad Khan, had arrived at the scene. Isa Mian announced that he had been forced to act in this way because he was wronged in the first instance. He threatened that if Bibi Jan was not given back to him, he would kill the boys.

The assembled persons tried, from threats to pleas, but nothing worked. A prominent banker of Lucknow, Govind Lal Sahu, even offered to give a written undertaking for any amount needed to spare the lives of the boys, but this too failed.

The worried Agha Mir rushed to the Residency and appealed to the Resident, Mr M. Ricketts, to help him. Ricketts agreed to intervene and sent Captain Locket for negotiations on the condition that the Captain be given a free hand in the matter and full support of both the Nawab and Agha Mir.

An unarmed Captain Locket was allowed inside the palace for negotiations. Isa Mian told him that Agha Mir had lowered his prestige in Lucknow by taking away from him his love, Bibi Jan. He said he would prefer death over dishonour. In return for the boys, he demanded that he be given back the custody of Bibi Jan, protection to his life and property, and Rs 5 lakhs. Captain Locket reminded him that his insistence on money would make people think that the issue he had made of self-respect was simply an excuse to extort money. This had the desired effect on Isa Mian, and he dropped the condition of money; the remaining conditions were written and accepted by the Captain.

At the end, as per the agreement, the boys were released and sent to their mother. According to an earlier promise made by Agha Mir in the morning, Rs 20,000 was brought to the maktab, as was Bibi Jan, to be handed over to Isa Mian. Bibi Jan was very nervous. But to the pleasant surprise of everyone, Isa Mian gave the courtesan Rs 1,000, and with a smile said, 'Now you are free from me and can go anywhere you wish.'

The Banke of Lucknow

In and around Lucknow, the younger generation still uses a Hindi word 'bakait', which means a person who loves to flaunt his muscle power. Apparently the word is the corrupt form of 'banka', a word used for a man, who, under the influence of Nawabi culture, acts chivalrously and honours his word.

Banke (plural of banka) were an intrinsic part of Lucknowi culture. Generally, they came from middle or lower income strata of the society. They never wore warm clothes in winter, to show that they were strong and tough enough to brave the vagaries of the weather. They could be seen only in kurtas of fine muslin, even on the coldest days of the season. Banke usually had highly volatile temperaments and were ready to fight at the drop of a hat. Self-respecting to a fault, guided by their king-size ego, they intentionally wore ghetto shoes (long, pointed, embroidered shoes), specially made in Lucknow, which were uncomfortable, and hence unsuitable for a hasty getaway, to convey the message that they were not interested in running away.

And in the face of certain defeat, they maintained their dignity. They grew their hair long, so that if they were killed, the enemy would not be able to lift their head by the ears.

The influence banke asserted in that society can be estimated by the fact that a bridge connecting the Chowk and Mansoor Nagar is known by Banke Ghulam Hussain.

It is said that Ghulam Hussain had such a reputation as a man who always kept his word, that once when he approached a moneylender with a small box to be mortgaged, the moneylender did not even care to see the contents of the box. After the loan was repaid, when Ghulam Hussain opened the box in the presence of everyone including the moneylender, it only had a hair of his moustache in it.

Lucknow's Darker Side

Many considered Lucknow under Nawabi rule as the richest city of its time. It was believed that it was even richer than the Presidencies of Calcutta, Bombay and Madras. Here, the fertile agricultural plains of Awadh generated much more revenue for the Nawabs than anywhere else. With all this wealth at their disposal and no worries about having to defend their boundaries — Awadh was protected by the British as per an agreement after they won the battle of Buxar against Nawab Shuja-ud-daulah — the Nawabs lived comfortably.

The richest rulers of their time, the Nawabs of Lucknow began creating a world of their own which suited their comforts, fancy and whims. This fabulous world consisted of magnificent, opulent buildings, charming courtesans, assemblies of famous poets, talented singers, and expert cooks.

However, there existed concurrently, another world in Lucknow; a world very different from the decadent culture of the palaces. Although historians prefer to ignore this section of people while writing their records, focusing instead on the handful of wealthy, with the help of accounts by foreign visitors of that time we can get some insight into how this other side lived. Reverend William writes in his *Indian Recreations*: 'Among all this blaze of wealth and magnificence, thousands of poor wretches are seen on the road, to all appearance in real want. There is not, perhaps in the whole compass of human affairs a more striking display of inequality of condition than this scene affords. Extravagant wealth is amassed in the hands of one man, and is confined in the narrow circle of his favourites; and his superfluous store is grinded from the faces of the indigent, who are wallowing in all the filth, of penury and wretchedness.'

Another keen observer, Major E.C. Archer, relates in *Tours in Upper India* and in *Parts of the Himalaya Mountains*, an incident that he witnessed in 1827: 'Men, women and children throwing themselves under the elephants to catch the pieces of money distributed by the nobleman who sat behind in the King's howdah [seat]. Those who did manage to pick up the heavy silver rupees... were often forced to surrender them to others more desperate'.

Lady Nugent could not stop herself from commenting in *A Journal from the Year 1811 till the Year 1815*: 'Impossible not to compare ostentation and splendour of the Nawab's procession with the half starved miserable appearance of his subjects'.

We do not find much on poverty by Indian writers except by Kamal-ud-din Haider and Mirza Abu Talib Khan. Both writers had to suffer for their comments. It might be that native writers were scared of royal wrath.

The Sport of Quail-Fighting

The meat of quail has always been considered a delicacy fit for royalty all over the India. The Nawabs of Lucknow, however, enjoyed quail in a different way — by watching them fight. Although the sport was enjoyed by many Nawabs of Lucknow, Nawab Nasir-ud-din Haidar evinced special interest it. According to Abdul Halim Sharar, author of *Guzishta Lakhnau*, Nasir-ud-din was inordinately fond of watching quails fight on his table.

Quail fighting or bater bazi is believed to have been introduced in Lucknow by the ancestors of renowned courtesans who had migrated from the Punjab during the rule of Nawab Saadat Ali Khan. As quail fighting did not require a large area or even a very long period of time, it was possible to organise this game at the houses of the elite.

Although many varieties of quails were available in the region, experts preferred the button quail. While taming and training the bird, apart from other time-tested methods, trainers whetted their beaks with penknives to make them more lethal.

There were a few quail owners who adopted unethical practices. They applied poisonous oil on the beaks of their quails; the opponent bird would then run away in the middle of a fight or later die of poisoning. There were others who fed their quail intoxicants before the fight so that the bird, oblivious of its wounds, would keep fighting. It is on record that an expert at preparing intoxicating pills for birds was so sought after, that he would sell each pill for as much as Rs 10.

To start a fight between the quails, grain was spread on the ground, and the birds then released. Quails have a tendency to attack each other on the head with their beaks and claws. Generally these quail-fights were decided within twenty minutes, after which time the weaker quail usually ran away from the fight. A large amount of money was lost or won in betting on these fights. Quail-fighters like Khwaja Hasan Chhanga, Mir Amdu and Mir Abid were well known for their skills.

The terminology used in quail fights was unique. When a newly-trained quail fought successfully in the first season, it was called Nau Kar when it appeared for its second season. If the same quail had another successful season, it was called Kuriz in its third season.

Quail owners were very proud of their birds and this was the reason they gave them grand names like Shohra-e-Afaq, which means 'world-famous', or Sohrab, the protagonist of the Persian epic *Shah Nameh*.

Why the Nawab Wanted to Kill his Son

The British had a very well-woven intelligence network to collect information about rulers who mattered to them. And often they manipulated this information to their own advantage. One of the rulers they gathered information about was Nawab Asif-ud-daulah. According to British historians, Nawab Asif-ud-daulah, the builder of the magnificent Asifi Imambara, got drunk 'like a beast' every night. The Nawab was said to prefer boys and even had a 'harem of boys'. And it was for this reason, that his wife remained a virgin.

Johan Pemble, a research fellow from the University of Leicester, offers evidence for the prevalence of a homoerotic culture and Asif-ud-daulah's predilection for it: 'The existence of male brothels is confirmed by the Lucknow Hospital report for 1848-49,' he has written, adding further, 'These practices had been made fashionable by the Nawab Asif-ud-daulah, a notorious catamite.'

In *A Very Ingenious Man: Claude Martin in Early Colonial India*, well-known British historian Rosie Llewellyn-Jones cautiously quotes from a private report sent to the Governor-General of India, Warren Hastings, about Nawab Asif-ud-daulah: 'Mirza Amani [Nawab Asif-ud-daulah] is one of those characters who dishonour human nature. His person [is] extremely disagreeable and his mind depraved beyond description. He is endowed with no capacity for business and abandoned to the most unnatural passions.'

She goes on to claim that Asif-ud-daulah was both a homosexual and pederast and that his wife remained a virgin years after their marriage.

Other Europeans who visited the court reported that, besides the fact that the 'new Nawab was so fat he was unable to mount a horse', that nowhere else could one find 'such example of depravity than those with which this man regaled his court and his capital every day. He was perpetually intoxicated with liquor. His evenings are generally devoted to his orderlies and his bottle... all appearance of decency and decorum is banished.'

Llewellyn-Jones explains in her book that, after becoming the ruler, one of the first things that Asif-ud-daulah did was to sack his father's ministers and to appoint his drinking companions to positions of power (like the distant relative, Murtaza Khan, who was thus elevated). She says the British Resident reported that, even while on tour in Awadh, the two men 'render themselves and the whole Court utterly incapable of business by getting drunk like beasts'.

While admitting that the British reports are biased, Llewellyn-Jones is unable to resist the temptation to add: 'It is said that Shuja-ud-daulah [Asif-ud-daulah's father], on learning of his son's sexual inclinations, would have had him put to death, had it not been for the intervention of his wife the Bahu Begum, Asif-ud-daulah's mother.'

Whether the Nawab was a homosexual or not, can be debated, but certain other records too indicate that young boys were 'used' in the society for paedophiliac activities till the end of the Nawabi era, and perhaps even later. For instance, as per a hospital report of February 1850, female prostitutes were often infected with venereal disease, and young boys aged between twelve and sixteen years were treated for syphilis. The occurrence of these diseases was ascribed to 'revolting practices' by the Superintendent Dr Leckie, who observes, 'there are Houses in the city, where... boys are professedly kept for above unnatural purpose.'

La Martiniere

Perhaps the only thing stranger than human nature in the world is the way a society pays its debt to a person who has done much for it. And nothing illustrates this better than the case of Claude Martin. A man of French origin, Martin joined the East India Company as a common soldier and by his sheer determination worked his way to the top.

Martin, who was great lover of art, joined Nawab Shuja-ud-daulah around 1774 at Faizabad as a political and military advisor. Later he made a great fortune in trade and the construction and sale of buildings to the Nawabs. This enabled him to maintain a lavish lifestyle. He had a good number of servants, many eunuchs and four concubines, which was regarded as a status symbol in those days. Besides, he had a personal collection of around four thousand books. A few of the books were in Sanskrit and Persian, indicating the range of his taste. Claude Martin was keenly interested in the arts and had a good collection of miniatures. He was fond of cockfighting too. It is said that he also made money by betting in cockfights with Nawab Saadat Ali Khan.

Martin shifted to Lucknow in 1776, during the time of Nawab Asif-ud-daulah. He planned to construct the most magnificent building of that period in Lucknow. He showed the plans of the proposed building to Nawab Asif-ud-daulah, who was responsible for the construction of the great Bara Imambara. The Nawab was so impressed by the plans that he offered to purchase it at the price of 10 lakhs gold coins. Unfortunately, before the deal could be finalised, the Nawab passed away. General Claude Martin went ahead with his plans and constructed the building himself; he named it Constantia, after a woman, Constance, that he was in love with in France.

The wealthy Claude Martin was a farsighted person. Since he had no children or legal heirs, he made arrangements that, after his death, he should be buried in the Constantia so that the building could not be taken away by any Nawab in the future. He also willed that three schools for orphans be opened with money from his properties. Two of these schools were in India — one at Lucknow and the other at Calcutta — and the third was in Lyons, France. He also willed that the building Constantia be converted into a hostel.

After his death, books from his library were auctioned in Lucknow; the rest of the estate was brought under the hammer in Calcutta in 1801.

As per his will, one school for orphans was started in 1836 in Calcutta, the other in Lucknow in 1840. Constantia was converted into a hostel, and after sometime, the school was shifted to Constantia, renamed La Martiniere.

Claude Martin did not intend that boys of any particular community be given preference. Unfortunately, in the first war of independence, freedom-fighters raided La Martiniere, dug up Martin's grave, and threw his bones all around the place. Later, when the British regained the place, they found one of these bones, which they again buried in its original spot. It is presumed that this might have been the reason why the British initially restricted the admission of Indian children to this school.

Today the school has become a premier and prestigious educational institute of Lucknow. It is ironical, however, that a school originally meant for orphans, is now accessible only to children of the elite.

The Prince's Punishment

Nawab Safdar Jung, the second ruler of Awadh, was different from other rulers of the Awadh dynasty in that he had only one wife, to whom he was totally dedicated. Ghulam Ali writes in his famous book *Imad-us-Saadat*, 'His natural modesty and sense of good conduct did not make him desire the company of any other woman except that of the illustrious and chaste lady [his wife Sadri-i-Jahan].' In A.L. Shrivastava's *The First Two Nawabs of Awadh*, Safdarjung is cited to have been perhaps the only Nawab 'whose private life was marked by a high standard of morality, extremely rare in the class [to] which he belonged to and in the age in which he lived'. Unfortunately, the lifestyle of his first-born son Shuja-ud-daulah, was in direct contrast to that of his father. While Shujauddaulah was still a prince, he began showing an inclination towards a permissive lifestyle.

The prince, who later became the third ruler of Awadh, is described by writers like Dow Alexander, George Forester, Sultan Ali Safauvi and A.L. Srivastava, as a strong and extremely handsome person. Once, unable to resist the charms of a young girl, he tried to climb into her room at night, but was caught. The girl's family reported the crime to the Kotwal, a senior law enforcer, who did not know how to deal with the royal prisoner. He awakened the Nawab to find out what he should do. Flaring up the moment he heard the entire story, the Nawab shot back, 'Had you been equal to your office, you would not have awakened me at midnight to ask me what is to be done with rascals that are escalading a citizen's house'.

The prince turned to his mother for help, but she not only refused to oblige, she also chastised him saying, 'Had I a son, that son would not attempt to rob a citizen of his honour. Let this son of a whore look for his mother in some caravan sarai.'

As the famous work *Seir-ul-Mutakhirin* has it, the prince, like other ordinary criminals, was confined to a loathsome place for a week. Once his term was over, the prince — famished and still in dirty clothes — was produced before Safdar Jung. The Nawab was playing chess. He casually looked up at his son and said sarcastically, 'So sir, it is you,' and then resumed his game.

After this episode, the prince's mother and father did not talk to him for six months despite his apologies. After six months, on his wife's recommendation, the Nawab talked to his son only once. It took another six months for the Nawab to normalise relations with his son.

What Wine Meant to Different Nawabs

One of the most culturally evolved Nawabs of Awadh, Nawab Wajid Ali Shah, was also one of the most misunderstood rulers of history, largely due to the British's version of how he administered the State. The British, with the eventual goal of annexing Awadh in mind, defamed this maestro of art, culture and literature.

The British portrayed his administration as a complete failure and him as a symbol of decadence, someone always indulging his appetite for spectacle, wine and women. Fed on these stories, even native historians tended to endorse the British point of view. However, Wajid Ali Shah was, in fact, a complete teetotaller.

For the most religious ruler of Awadh, the tenth Nawab, Amjad Ali Shah, wine meant sin. As per the accounts of German traveller Von Orlich, when the British Resident invited Amjad Ali Shah for breakfast or dinner, his own servants accompanied him. He would drink only tea and leave when the English started dancing.

Though wine was anaethema for the last two Nawabs of the Awadh dynasty — Amjad Ali and his son Wajid Ali — other Nawabs suffered from no such aversion.

The fourth Nawab, Asif-ud-daulah, was extremely fond of bhang and wine. After shifting his capital from Faizabad to Lucknow, one of the first things he did was to request the then Governor-General of India, Warren Hastings, to send him a stock of different kinds of wine from Calcutta. In the letter written in Persian to Warren Hastings, he wrote that he was 'fond of wine'.

The British Resident, Johan Bristow, while reporting on a hunting party of Asif-ud-daulah in 1776 at Etawa, painted Asif-ud-daulah's drinking parties in a very negative light. The Resident insinuated that Asif-u-ddaulah was incapable of conducting business because of his drinking habits.

The sixth Nawab, Saadat Ali Khan, also enjoyed wine, but his only regret was that he was too generous a host under its influence. It is reported that he used to generously hand out gifts when he was drunk, and immediately repent his largesse when sober.

The first king and the seventh Nawab, Ghazi-ud-din Haidar, was also a connoisseur of wine and enjoyed it during musical sittings.

His successor, Nasir-ud-din Haidar, was a compulsive drinker. He was easily manipulated when intoxicated, a fact that his courtiers, including George Harris Derusett, took advantage of.

How Ghararas came to be worn in Lucknow

Churidar pyjamas are an intrinsic part of our attire. And although we have been involved with the constant evolution in how they are worn, in fact, they did not originate in our land.

This dress, so suited to our climate, came with the Muslim conquerors to our country. It used to be the standard dress at the court of Baghdad and later became popular in Turkey and Persia. The earlier pyjamas resembled the sharai pyjamas, but its style and design continued to change according to time, taste and region. For example, people from the Qandhar region of Afghanistan and recruited into the Delhi's Mughal army, wore wide-legged pyjamas. These mercenaries from Qandhar were considered very brave soldiers, so people from Delhi took to copying their attire, including the pyjamas they wore.

In Lucknow, churidar pyjamas were introduced in a very unusual way. During the Nawabi era, the native army of Awadh along with the British army fought against the Sikhs in the Punjab. The Awadhi army noticed that the Sikhs wore tight pyjamas — called ghutannas — which were designed by cutting cloth on the bias. The style caught the Awadhi army's fancy, and it was these men who brought it back to Awadh. Churidar pyjamas, too, are designed on the lines of ghutannas.

One of the most sensuous female costumes, the gharara, owes its popularity in Lucknow to the eighth ruler of Awadh, Nasir-ud-din Haidar. This Nawab, who ruled between 1827 and 1837, was very influenced by European culture and tried to emulate that lifestyle. He himself often wore Western clothes. He noticed some similarity between the gharara and the evening gown that British women wore, and so he made all the royal women in his palace wear ghararas.

Beneficiaries of the Nawabs' Wealth

The Nawabs had set up a unique financial system, under which a considerable sum was deposited as a loan with the East India Company and nominated persons and their heirs received regular monthly income from the interest on this amount. This political pension was called wasiqa. The wasiqa paid to close relatives of former rulers from the Nawabs' native land was known as amanat, and the pension paid to the commoners was called zamanat.

The main beneficiaries of this scheme tended to be Shia families. Since the Awadh dynasty were Shias by religion, this regal association meant a higher social standing for the Shias over other religious groups. It was to be expected that Shia families and institutions prospered under the Nawabs. Unusually, however, even after the death of the last Nawab, these families and their heirs continued receiving financial support. It was because of this arrangement, that the Shia nobility not only survived but also comfortably maintained its financial status much after the end of Nawabi rule.

One of the richest begums of the Awadh dynasty was the wife of the third Nawab, Shuja-ud-dalauh, and mother of Asif-ud-daulah. She had given a huge amount of money and property to the East India Company under this system, which yielded an annual income of Rs 10,000. This income was used as pension for persons nominated by her.

Shiekh Tassuddeque Hussain records that, in the year 1825, the first king of Awadh, Ghazi-ud-din Haidar, gave one crore rupees to the East India Company at an interest rate of five percent. The deal he executed with the Company was that a pension of Rs 10,000 would be paid to his begum, Mubarak Mahal, Rs 2,500 to Mariam Begum, Rs 11,000 to Mumtaz Mahal, and Rs 1,000 per month to Sarfaraz Begum. It was incorporated in the deal, that after the death of these begums, their nominees would be entitled to only one-third the amount; the remaining two-third would be spent on different charitable and religious projects.

Ghazi-ud-din Haidar also made provision from this amount to provide for the maintenance of the Imambara Shah Najaf built by him, and where at last he was buried with his four wives.

King Nasir-ud-din Haider, Ghazi-ud-din Haider's son, followed in his father's footsteps and gave a loan of Rs 62.40 lakh to the British at the same interest rate of five percent. The interest was to be paid as pension of Rs 6,000 to Nawab Taj Mahal, Rs 6,000 to Nawab Mukhadr Alia, Rs 10,000 to Malka Zamania, and Rs 4,000 per month to his stepdaughter Nawab Sultan Alia, daughter of his wife, Malka Zamania, from her first husband.

According to author Saffdar Hussain, in 1838, the ninth Nawab, Mohammad Ali Shah, deposited Rs 7 lakh with the East India Company to pay pension from the accruing interest to his wives and their descendants and dependants. Mohammad Ali Shah promoted and preserved the architectural heritage of Awadh. He set up a fund of Rs 36 lakh for the upkeep of quite a few Nawabi buildings and the celebration of Muharram at these places. This fund met the maintenance expenses of the Hussainabad Imambara built by him, the Asifi Imambara built by Asif-ud-daulah, and the mausoleum of Saadat Ali Khan. Construction began on the Jama Masjid during Mohammad Ali Shah's reign; after his death, his wife Malka-e-Jahan ensured that it was completed. She too benefited under this fund.

Col W.H. Sleeman mentions that the tenth Nawab, Amjad Ali Shah, gave the British a sum of Rs 18,30,000 to invest in Government notes; his several wives were regularly given a pension out of the interest on this amount.

Wasiqa helped the Shia nobility maintain their status after

the Nawabs' demise, but not for very long. As every good thing must come to an end, so did wasiqa: with the passage of time, the amount got diluted because of the increasing number of claimants in each generation.

Nowadays, what the majority of wasiqa-holders get is a ridiculously paltry amount. However, even to this day its claimants do collect this money from the wasiqa office, although, in many cases, the actual amount might be less than the claimant's conveyance costs. For them, the mere collection of their claim is a matter of pride and an assertion of their blue-blooded lineage.

Maulvis in Lucknow

During the time of the Nawabs, the Shia Ulama were respected and influential to such a degree that even the Nawabs avoided any confrontation with them. Maulvi Dildar Ali and his son, Maulana Sayed Mohammad, were particularly powerful Ulama.

Born in Rae Bareilly district, Dildar Ali had studied Shia theology at Najaf Ashraf in Iraq. A religious reformer, he is credited with organising the Shias and standardising their rituals according to Shia doctrines.

On 12 May 1786, he led the first Shia namaz in jamat (congregation), and later, on 26 May 1786, he led the Friday congregational prayer, said to be the first public congregation in northern India. It is believed that Nawab Asif-ud-daulah, who was the first to publicly patronise the Shia sect, gave up using bhang (an intoxicant) after hearing his sermons.

Dildar Ali's eldest son, Maulana Sayed Mohammad, was a great scholar too, as well as a popular figure. He never differentiated between the commoners and the king. Once, when Nawab Nasir-ud-din Haider, who ascended the throne on 20 October 1827, fell for the charms of a married woman and wanted to marry her, Maulana Sayed Mohammad refused to perform their nikah (marriage) on the grounds that her husband had not formally released her.

The Maulana also had the courage to deny religious sanction to Nasir-ud-din's habit of drinking, which he did citing medical grounds.

The Maulana had very close and cordial relations with King Mohammad Ali, yet he refused to lead the prayer in the newly constructed Jama Masjid of Hussainabad, as a portion of the mosque had encroached on private land. Only when the king agreed to find a solution to the problem and Maulana convinced the owner to accept compensation for the land, did the Maulana lead the prayer.

The Maulana certainly deserved the title of 'Sultan-ul-Ulama' (King of the Learned), given to him by Nawab Amjad Ali.

Maulvi Dildar Ali, who standardised Shia rituals in India

Sultan-ul-Ulama

Why Lucknow's Kababs are so Soft

The Nawabs had a great weakness for food and attached immense importance to their kitchen and staff. In fact, two khansamans (supervisor/cook) of royal kitchens were later promoted to the post of prime minister of Awadh! One of them was the khansaman of Nawab Shuja-ud-daulah, Hasan Reza Khan, popularly called Mirza Hasanau. He was appointed as prime minister by Shuja-ud-daulah's successor, Asif-ud-daulah, with the title of 'Sarfaraz-ud-daulah'. The other was Agha Mir, the khansaman of the sixth ruler, Nawab Saadat Ali Khan, who was appointed prime minister by the seventh ruler, Nawab Ghazi-ud-din Hadar.

The Nawabs' kitchen expenses were exorbitant. For example, Nawab Shuja-ud-daulah's kitchen expenses — excluding staff salaries — was Rs 2,000 per day. He was served from six different kitchens every day, including one of his mother's, and one of his wife's. (In those days, it was the practice in royal households to send food to each other as a sign of regard.) Nawab Asif-ud-daulah — who built the Asafi Imambara — spent more on food than on his thousands of elephants. It is said that Salar Jang — a brother of Bahu Begum — paid one of his cooks a salary of Rs 1,200 per month, the highest in India.

Royal patronage provided an excellent opportunity for the cooks to experiment, as a result of which a new style of cooking — later called 'Awadhi' was evolved. This cuisine is a rare blend of Mughal and Persian cooking, as the Nawabs of Awadh, who were originally from Iran, were part of the Mughal Empire.

The Nawabs loved eating the different kinds of food prepared by their expert chefs so much that it often adversely affected their teeth. It is believed among the families of Lucknow's traditional chefs, that the kababs of Lucknow are exceptionally soft because most Nawabs had bad teeth. This story is endorsed by a report made by a Captain Madan, in which he describes Asif-ud-daulah: 'Though a young man he [has] lost all his teeth, this makes him splutter in speaking, which he does without ceasing'.

A Religious and Fashion Statement

Headwear is often a projection of the culture and the ideology of a people. The same was true in Awadh. Often, what began as a religious statement became fashionable among the public.

For example, in the time of Nawab Nasir-ud-din Haidar, when Shia religion and culture dominated in society, Nasir-ud-din got a five-cornered cap designed for himself to show his regard for the five members of the Prophet's family. It was strictly meant for the king and no one else was allowed to wear this cap. After his death, however, the general public began to use this cap in place of the four-cornered chau goshia cap, which had been in use earlier. The five-cornered cap became very popular in Lucknow, and later on, so much delicate chikan embroidery was used to decorate it that it would take a year to produce one cap.

But ideology and fashion both change with time: when a prince from Delhi came to live in Lucknow, his dopalli cap took the fancy of the common man. Prepared by stitching two pieces of cloth, they were easy to make and light to wear. Because of his cap, this prince was called 'prince of dopalli cap'. Later on, with some improvements on the dopalli cap, a nukka dar cap was designed, which was pointed on the front and back. The affluent wore this cap with embroidery done in silver and gold.

During Ghazi-ud-din Haidar's reign, a cap shaped like a tambourine, called mandel, was so popular at court that people who were not wearing a pagri or mandel cap were not allowed to meet the king or princes. After some time, the topi — more rounded at the forehead and back of the head — evolved from the mandel cap. It was additionally attractive because it resembled the caps worn by soldiers of the British army.

Nawab Saadat Ali Khan — who was the first Nawab to

discontinue the drooping style of moustache — also adopted a new style of pagri called shimla by the locals.

The last and the most creative Nawab of Lucknow, Wajid Ali Shah, created a cap with a cardboard base called alam pasand, meaning 'world pleasing'. It was meant for those who had been honoured with important titles. But this cap failed to be become popular even in his lifetime.

Wajid Ali Shah's Premonition

Coincidences visit the lives of both commoners and kings. The last Nawab of the Awadh dynasty, Wajid Ali Shah, had a very strange experience when he was living on government pension at Matia Burj in Calcutta.

Lord Mayo, who was appointed the Viceroy of India in 1869, wanted to meet the Nawab. As S. Ameer Ali Khan notes in his book, *Wazeernamah*, 'It was generally talked about in Matia Burj, that [it was] Lord Mayo [who] first called on the King.' Wajid Ali Shah was much pleased by this friendly gesture of the Viceroy, and as per protocol, he paid a return visit the very next day.

At Government House, the official residence of the Viceroy, Lord Mayo received Wajid Ali in the Throne Room. The Viceroy sat with him in this room and had a formal but cordial conversation with the Nawab. All of sudden, no one knows what motivated him, the Viceroy got up from his chair, which was next to the Nawab's, and sat on the Presidential Chair, which was placed on a balcony called 'Shah-nasheen'. The Viceroy was now sitting at a higher level than the Nawab.

Nawab Wajid Ali was so hurt by Lord Mayo's act, that he immediately got up and left the Throne Room, without a word to the Viceroy.

Once he arrived at his palace at Matia Burj, someone from his inner circle asked him why he had left the Government House without formally taking leave of the host, the Viceroy. At this, Wajid Ali replied, 'To whom could I [have] bid farewell? I saw a corpse lying on that high Presidential chair instead of a living person.'

Within a few months of this episode, in February 1876, Lord

Mayo was killed by a convict during the last leg of his tour of Andaman Islands.

For most people, it was mere coincidence, but devoted admirers of Wajid Ali Shah preferred to believe that it was supernatural insight that helped the Nawab foresee the Viceroy's death.

How Chikan came to Lucknow

The work of a good craftsman is always appreciated, and in Lucknow, none more so than those who are experts in the world-renowned chikankari work. In fact, the profession has always been so respected, that it is one vocation that affluent families have been able to take up without any perceived loss of societal acceptance.

It is said that one of the wives of a Nawab belonged to Mursidabad in Bengal where chikan work was established and popular at that time. While in the harem, she did not have much to do, so, to keep herself busy, she embroidered a cap belonging to the Nawab with chikan work. He was very pleased, and seeing this, the other begums picked up this craft to impress the Nawab. Thus, chikan embroidery became associated with the upper class. And that is the reason why ladies from affluent and royal families, in the time of crises, did not hesitate to take up this work to support their families.

Although, according to this version, chikankari came to Lucknow from Mursidabad, it blossomed with the refining influence of the culture of the Nawabs. As a result, there is the striking difference between the chikan work of Bengal and that of Lucknow. The former caters to the masses, and the latter to the classes. It is said that exceptionally good Lucknow chikan work on a garment could get, in those days, a worker enough money to feed his family for one full year.

As per another version, Nur Jahan, the wife of Emperor Jahangir, saw the beautiful motifs of the royal buildings in Iran. She liked it so much that she asked her staff to create the same patterns on her clothes. And when one of her royal staff members, Begum Bismillah, came to Lucknow, this craft became popular here too. In both the cases, the patrons and practitioners were from the upper class.

Chikankari is the art of creating fascinating motifs on the cloth with stitches. In the past, there were as many as thirty-two kinds of stitches, but most of them are no longer in use. Now, there are primarily murry, phanda, shadow, jali, tepchi and hatkati. Each one of these is used for a different purpose, and this is what makes chikankari unique.

Chikan Work

Hair as a Fashion Statement

Change and variety are the spice of life and fast changing fashion trends simply endorse this characteristic of human beings. And in the area of fashion, the most experimented on part of body is the hair.

The first Nawab of Awadh, Saadat Khan, sported a well-trimmed beard. But the third Nawab Shuja-ud-daulah, like Emperor Akbar, did not like facial hair, and so got rid of it. This changed the trend in Lucknow and after him all the nobles of Lucknow shied away from sporting a beard.

As people in power and position invariably set trends in fashion, commoners — especially Shias — stopped sporting beards. And with no hair available on their cheeks, a good number of people tried to be creative with their sideburns, by keeping these thick or thin and stretching them to different length and shapes.

Those men who still wore beards, tried to adopt similar styles as those of Hindu and Rajput soldiers. In this style, the beard was parted at the chin and lifted up to the ears on both the sides.

The first Muslims who came to India, by and large, either had the hair of their head shaved off or had very short hair, which they covered with ammamas, a kind of cap. But the long hair of Hindus fascinated them, so they imitated this style. Royals from Delhi, who made Lucknow their permanent home, introduced this trend there. Residents of Lucknow adopted it, but not without adding changes of their own.

Apart from other styles, the young people of Lucknow were so fascinated by the hairstyles of women that they copied them, and began wearing their hair wavy. When the women switched over to the British way of combing their hair back and keeping the forehead bare, a good number of men adopted the style.

Settling Scores in the Sky

The popularity of games and sports changes with social conditions, time and taste. However, there are a few sports, which have survived for centuries. Kite fighting is one of such sport.

Initially, people did not indulge in kite-fighting. They used to take pride in flying different kinds of kites and tried to outsmart each other by flying innovative kinds of kites. Some people flew kites at night with an oil-soaked cloth hung by a wire attached to the kites and set alight. Others flew kites in the shape of human figures. However, with the passage of time, people began enjoying cutting the cords of other kites with their own. With this began the sport of kite-fighting with all its complicated skills, and people started betting money on it.

One interesting characteristic that this game had in Nawabi Lucknow, is the looting of a fallen kite. This goes back to the fourth Nawab, Asif-ud-daulah, who had imparted grandeur to this sport. His kites, called tukkals in the local language, were decorated with fringes of silver and gold equal to Rs 5, a sum that was a fortune in those days. Anyone who looted a kite could either collect the Rs 5 in exchange for the kite from the Nawab's staff, or simply sell it in the market for almost the same amount.

Master kite-fighters commanded respect in those days. Sheikh Imdad, Mir Amdu and Khwaja Mathan were some of those whose kite-fighting exploits spread far and wide. The tukkal kite of Asif-ud-daulah's time was a bit complicated as it was made of two bows and one back-stick. By the time of the tenth Nawab, Amjad Ali, a simple kite called guddi was evolved. It had only one bow and one back-stick and its shape was like an upright diamond. During the reign of Wajid Ali Shah, kites with one-and-a-half bows and one back-stick were prepared and this shape continued till the post-Nawabi period.

After this, Ustad Agha Abu Turab Khan, from the family of Salar Jang, and a few other noble men, styled a kite with a patta, a paper triangle in place of the tassel at the bottom. Kites with pattas were known as kankawwa, and with tassel, dehr kana. These shapes are now popular throughout the country.

There are two styles of kite-fighting. The Khinch style involves tugging and reeling in the cord in a quick motion, and the other, Bada, entails slackening the cord by slowly reeling it out, and letting the kite take its own course. In Lucknow, Bada was in fashion among the royals, as it required a considerable length of cord. However, later on, Khinch became popular. Kite-fighting matches are still known as Bada in Lucknow, in which people gain or lose heavy amounts of money. The most important day of the year for a kite-flyer is Jamghat. It falls a day after Diwali, and as a tradition, the young and the old kite-fighters spend the day under the sky as kites spar overhead.

Begging — a Big Business

During the reign of Nawab Naisr-ud-din Haider, between 20 October 1827 and 8 July 1837, carrying several weapons and sporting a bushy moustache and beard were a popular trend.

Generally, a man would carry a rifle, a pistol and a sword along with a shield made of buffalo leather. Even people dressed in worn-out clothes and engaged in the most ordinary vocations in life carried at least one sword and dangled a shield from their left shoulder. Children were given toy pistols, swords, bows and arrows to play with. It is not surprising then that, as a result, the largest number of soldiers in the service of the East India Company were recruited from Awadh.

Weapons also fascinated the beggars of Lucknow. Invariably, they were armed with all sorts of weapons. Displaying of arms in public was an act of pride for these beggars. The beggars of Awadh were arrogant when it came to their profession: if not obliged, they would in turn hurl the choicest expletives at the person. They kept a watch on the richer families of Lucknow: the moment a child was born, or a marriage was arranged, they demanded a sum from the celebrants. It was a common sight to find a group of beggars heckling a family for money.

How rewarding begging had become in those days, can be judged by the fact that one beggar in Lucknow was so prosperous, he rode on his pet elephant when he went out to beg from a few selected families.

Recreating Lucknow in Calcutta

When the last king of Awadh, Wajid Ali Shah, having lost his kingdom to the East India Company, left for Calcutta to plead his case with the Governor-General in 1856, hardly anyone, including the king himself, realised that he would create a new township in Calcutta on the lines of Lucknow and its culture.

After a long-drawn legal battle, the king resigned himself to his fate. He accepted the annual pension of Rs 12 lakh and a large piece of land allotted to him in exchange for his sovereignty.

About three to four miles to the south of Calcutta, there was a sleepy hamlet called Garden Ridge; because of a large mound of earth there, it was popularly known as Matia Burj (meaning mound of earth, in the local dialect). Situated on the bank of the Hoogly river, its total area was about six to seven miles, and it included a few palatial buildings. It was this land and buildings which were given to Wajid Ali Shah and his staff to live. Wajid Ali named the two main buildings into which he shifted Sultankhana and Aasud Manzil; he called a third one given to him Murssa Manzil.

In Lucknow, the king had constructed only a few building including a palace, Qaisarbagh, and a burial place for his father, the Sibtainabad Imambara. In Matia Burj, however, Wajid Ali constructed a row of palatial buildings including the Sultani, Shahanshah Manzil, Shah Manzil, Noor Manzil, Badami and Asmani Adalat Manzil. His buildings were always given Urdu or Persian names.

The population of this new township had by now reached 40,000. It consisted of magnificent mansions, well-maintained lush green lawns with all kind of plants, and even a zoo — one of a kind in this part of the world. It is said that the king once purchased a rare pair of pigeons for Rs 20,000 and a white peacock for Rs 11,000.

The entire area, encircled by high boundary wall, was divided by a mile-long road on either side of which were shops established by traders from Lucknow. Every kind of goods found in Lucknow was available in these shops, and the language of business was the chaste Urdu of Lucknow.

To keep time, a naubatkhana (a kind of bandstand) in the style of Awadh was constructed at the entrance of the main building, the Sultankhana. Here musicians played their instruments at regular intervals to announce the time of the day.

By this time, Lucknow was in the process of losing its charm because the singers, poets, dancers, tawaifs, animal keepers and other artistes who had comprised such an integral part of Lucknowi culture, had begun migrating from the city because of the lack of royal patronage. Wajid Ali Shah missed his Lucknow, and so he encouraged these artistes to migrate to Matia Burj, rewarding each of them generously when they did arrive. Thus the new township flourished in all respects along the lines of Lucknow.

Life in the township was like being in Lucknow itself: the residents spoke the same chaste Urdu; there were the same gatherings of singers and poets; mujras, dances, kite-flying and cock-fighting contests were organised. Even the opium addicts were to be found all around. In fact, the entire tangible and intangible culture was so much like Lucknow's, it was hard to believe that one was, in fact, hundreds of miles away from it, in Bengal. The Tazia procession of Wajid Ali Shah in Matia Burj was so grand, it is said that the best of Tazia processions in Nawabi Lucknow were no match to it.

Like every good thing, this too came to an end. Wajid Ali Shah died in 1887, and, between the rivalry among relatives to succeed the king and a lack of funds, everything that Wajid Ali Shah had built, collapsed. Like an illusion, everything was over.

Bibliography

Ahad, A., trans. by Ahmed, M.T. (1938) *Tarikh Badshah Begum*, Delhi.

Ali, M.M. *Observation on the Musulmans of India*, 2nd ed., London.

Alland, Z. (1987) *Traders and Nabobs*, UK: Michael Russell Publishing Ltd.

Archer, E.C. (1833) *Tour in Upper India and in Parts of the Himalayan Mountains*, London.

Azhar, M.A. (1982) *King Wajid Ali Shah of Awadh*, Karachi: Royal Book House.

Baksh, M.F. (1887) *Tarrikh-e-Farahbaksh*, trans. by W. Hoey as *Memoirs of Delhi and Faizabad*, Allahabad.

Bhatnagar G. D. (1968) *Awadh Under Wajid Ali Shaw*, Benares.

Edwardes, M. (1960) *The Orchid House*, London.

Edwardes, M. (1973) *Red Year: The Indian Rebellion of 1857*, London.

Egerton, F., *Journal, a Winter Tour in India*.

Gazetteers of Lucknow, ed H.R. Neville.

Ghulam, A. (1808) *Imad-us-Saadat*, Lucknow: N.K. Press.

Haidar, S.K. (1907) *Quaisar-ut-Tawareek*, 3rd ed. Lucknow: N.K. Press.

Haidar, S. K. (1907) *Sawanihat-i-Salatin-i-Awadh*, Lucknow: N.K. Press.

Hasan, A. (1983) *Palace Culture of Lucknow*, Delhi: B.R. Publishing Corporation.

Hay, S. (1939) *Historic Lucknow*, Delhi: Asian Educational Services.

Herber, B. (1829) *Narrative of Journey through the Upper Provinces of India from Calcutta to Bombay*, London.

Hibbert, C. (1978) *The Great Mutiny India 1857*, London: Allen Lane.

Husain, S.T. (1946) *Begamat-i-Awadh*, Lucknow.

Husani, S. (1975) *Lucknow Ki Tahjibi Miras*, Lahore.

Hussain, M.J. (1981) *Qadeem Lakhnaw Aj Kal*, New Delhi.

Information Department, Uttar Pradesh Government, *Naya Daur*, Lucknow.

Irwin, H.C. (1880) *The Garden of India*, London.

Jan, M. (1877) *Hadeeqa-e-Shuhada*.

Kashmiri, A.H. (2002), *Shahna Awadh Haqiqat Ki Aina Main*, Lucknow.

Khan, S.A.A. (1876) *Wazeernamah*, Lucknow: Nizami Press.

Khan, U.H. (1975) *Seir-ul-Mutakhirin*, Lahore.

Khanjar, F.A. (1934) *Mahal Khana-e-Shahi*, Lucknow: Nami Press.

Khayal M.T., *Bostan-e- Khayal*.

Knighton, W. (1921) *The Private Life of an Eastern King*, Oxford.

Llewellyn-Jones, R. (1985) *A Fatal Friendship: The Nawabs, The British and the City of Lucknow*, Oxford: Oxford University Press.

Llewellyn-Jones, R. (1999) *A Very Ingenious Man: Claude Martin in Early Colonial India*, Oxford: Oxford University Press.

Llewellyn-Jones, R. (2000) *Engaging Scoundrels: True Tales of Old Lucknow*, Oxford: Oxford University Press.

Low, U. (1936) *Fifty years with Johan Company*, London.

Lucas, S. (1971) *Dacoitee in Excelsis*, Lucknow.

Mehdi, M.A., trans. by Hoey, W. (1971) *Tarikh-i-Lucknow*, Lucknow.

Mehdi, M.A., *T'arikh-i-Sultan-ul-Ulema*, Lucknow.

Mehra, P. (1985) *A Dictionary of Modern Indian History 1707-1947*, Oxford: Oxford University Press.

Mill, J. (1826) *A History of British India*, London.

Mukherjee, P.C. (1983) *Pictorial Lucknow*, Lucknow.

Nugent, M. (1839) *A Journal from the Year 1811 to the Year 1815*, London.

Omar, M. *Hindustani Tahjib Ka Mussalmano Per Asar.*

Parkes, F. (1850) *Wanderings of a Pilgrim in Search of the Picturesque*, London.

Pemble, J. (1977) *The Raj, the Indian Mutiny and the Kingdom of Oudh 1801-1859*, Sussex: Harvester Press.

Qateel, M. (1968) *Haft Tamasha*, trans. Mohammad Umar.

Rampuri, M.N.G.(1919)*Tareekh-e-Awadh, N.K.Press, Lucknow.*

Records of U.P. State Museum, Lucknow.

Records of U.P. State Archives, Lucknow.

Russel, W.H. (1860) *My Diary in India in the year 1857-58*, London.

Santha, (1980) *Begums of Awadh*, Varanasi: Bharathi Prakashan.

Saxena, R.B. (1940) *A History of Urdu Literature*, Allahabad.

Shah, W.A., *Tarkikh-e-Parikhana.*

Sharar, A.H., *Guzishta Lakhnau,* trans. by Harcourt, E.S. and Husain, F. (1975) as *The Last Phase of Oriental Culture*, London.

Sharar, A.H., (1951) *Jan-e-Alam*, Lahore.

Sharma, S.K., *Nightfall of Mughal Empire in India.*

Shrivastava, A.L. (1933) *The First Two Kings of Oudh,* Lucknow: The Upper India Publishing House.

Singh, J. (2001) *Awadh ki Loot*, Delhi: National Publishing House.

Sleeman, W.H. (1850) *A Journey through the Kingdom of Oudh in 1849-50*, London: Pelhan Richardson.

Suroor, R.A.B. (1957) *Fasana-i-Ibrat*, Lucknow.

Talib, A., trans. by Hoey, W. (1971) *The History of Asifuddaulah*, Lucknow.

Tandon, B. (2001) *The Architecture of Lucknow and its Dependencies 1722-1856*, Delhi: Vikas Publishing House.

Valentia, G.V. (1809) *Voyages and Travels to India, Ceylon, The Red Sea, Abyssinia and Egypt*, London.

Von Orlich, L., trans. by Evans, H. (1845), *Travels in India Including Sindh and Punjab*, London.

White, *The Murdered King of Oudh*.

William, Tennant, (1804) *Indian Recreations*, London.

Woodiwiss A. ed. (1990) *Lawrence of Lucknow*, UK.

Glossary

Abad: populated

Aish: pleasure

Angiya: very short blouse

Bagh: garden

Bakshi: senior employee dealing with salary and other monetary affairs

Bater bazi: quail fighting

Begum: wives

Bhang: an intoxicant

Bungla: a kind of bungalow

Burra sahibs: higher level officers

Darbar: court

Daroga: chief supervisor

Dastarkhan: carpeted arrangement made for dining

Deras: tents

Diwan: one of the top courtiers

Dopahar: noon

Dupattas: a very long scarf commonly used by women

Faiza: profit

Fakir: beggar / religious beggar

Firangi: a native word used for British and other Europeans

Ghee: clarified butter

Gola: cannonball

Gopis: female cowherds

Imambara: residence for an Imam

Jamat: Islamic preaching session with one preacher and minimum two followers

Jagir: a piece of land or area given by a king

Kalidar painch: a special type of female costume for the lower part of the body

Kamdani: embroidery with thin wires

Kataars: small sword

Khalsa: personal land of the king

Khansamans: supervisor of store / cook / steward

Khasdans: betel dish

Khillat: robe of honour

Kotwal: a senior law enforcer

Kurti, kurta or saluki: a kind of long and loose costume for the upper part of the body

Lotas: copper vessels / a water pot

Mahal: wives / palace

Maktab: place of study

Mali: gardener

Masnad: cylindrical-shaped large pillow for support while sitting

Maulvis: teachers of Islam

Mir Atish: chief of artillery

Mohalla: locality

Mufti-e-Adalat: religious judge

Muhammadi Jhanda: Prophet Muhammad's standard, religious flag

Mujras: dance and song performances given by a tawaif

Mujtahid: Shia jurist

Mujtahidul Asr: present Shia religious jurist

Munazira: public debate between the Shia–Sunni sects

Mushairas: gatherings of poets for the recital of their poems in public

Muta: the Persian word for pleasure; in the Shia Muslim sect, Muta is a marriage for a particular time and usually for some monetary consideration

Naib: assistant

Namaaz: Islamic prayer

Naqqals: acrobats, mimics

Nath utarna: taking off the nose ring

Nauhas: mourning songs or verse

Nautch: dance

Nazar: gift

Nazim: Administrator of a particular area

Nikah: marriage by Islamic rituals

Paani: water

Pahar, ghari: system of time used previously; twenty-four hours were divided in eight pahars, each pahar was divided into eight gharis, one pahar was equal to three hours

Palang: bed

Palkis: palanquins

Panchayat: local governmental body

Parathas: Indian bread

Parganas: administrative division of an area

Pari: fairy

Pujas: worship ceremonies

Pulao: a preparation made of boiled rice and meat

Raja: King

Sadhu: ascetic

Seer: about a kilogram

Shabash: Bravo

Soz: mourning poems for Imam Hussain

Sozkhwan: singers of soz

Suba: province
Subedar: governor of a province
Tahsildar: administrative and revenue officer
Takhallus: pen-name
Takht: wooden bed
Tapka: a cloth belt
Tawaif: a high class prostitute who earns by singing and dancing
Tazia: a replica of a religious tomb made with paper and bamboo
Tazia-Dars: keepers of tazia
Tehzeeb: etiquette
Ulema: Islamic priest / scholar
Urad: a variety of lentil
Ustad: teacher / master
Vakeel: Lawyer
Vakil-i-mutlaq: fully authorised agent / procurer
Villayati: foreigner
Waseeka: a type of political pension
Wasil-baqi: Lawyer, retaining of access land tax
Wazir: minister
Zamindar: landlord / owner of land with some administrative powers

Index

Acknowledgements

I wish to thank the following institutes and their staff for permitting me to use their books, records, manuscripts, pictures and other source material, and for their support in many other ways.

Archaeological Survey of India
Amir-ud-daulah Public Library
Umadat-ul-Ulama Imambara Ghufran Maab
U. P. Urdu Academy
U. P. State Archives
U. P. State Museum
U. P. Sangeet Natak Academy
Directorate, U. P. State Archaeology
Directorate, U. P. Tourism
Indian Institute of Management
Tagore Library, University of Lucknow
Private Collections

I am extremely grateful to the editors of the *Times of India, Indian Express, Hindustan Times* and various other reputed newspapers who have given space for my regular columns related to the history of Awadh. This encouraged me to do further research in the area.

My mother, Savitri Di, herself the author of several books, has been a constant source of inspiration.

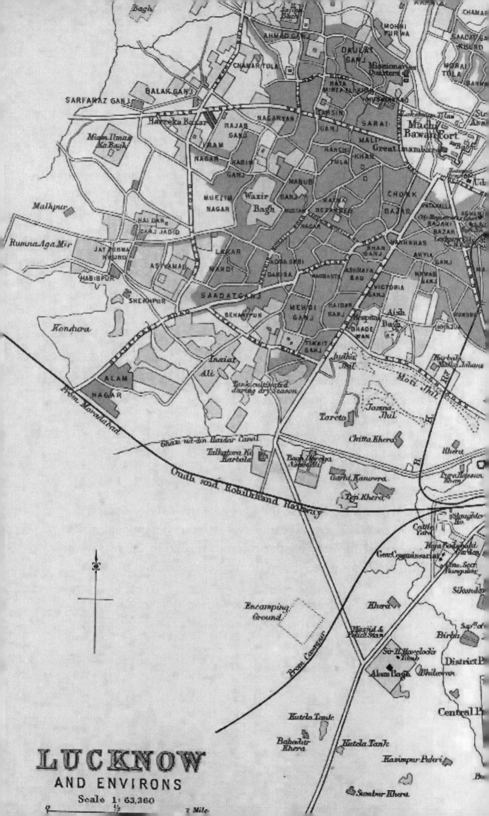

LUCKNOW
AND ENVIRONS
Scale 1 : 63,360